1 Thessalonians

a 6-lesson study containing

weekly commentary

and

daily study questions

by

Doris W. Greig

updated and revised by

Kathy Rowland

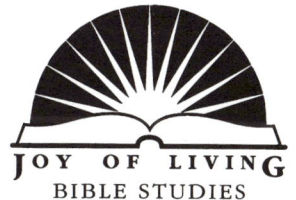

Published by Joy of Living Bible Studies
Printed in U.S.A.

For a free catalog please contact us at:

Joy of Living Bible Studies	800-999-2703 or 805-650-0838
2500 Knoll Dr., #G	website: www.joyofliving.org
Ventura, CA 93003	e-mail: info@joyofliving.org

This study was previously published in looseleaf format, © 1986, as part of the study titled *Multi-Book Study*, and has been revised and updated.

Unless otherwise noted, all Scripture quotations in these lessons are from the Holy Bible, *New International Version* (North American Edition). Copyright © 1973, 1978, 1984 by International Bible Society. Used by permission.

Also quoted is the *New American Standard Bible* (NASB), © Copyright The Lockman Foundation, 1960, 1962, 1963, 1968, 1971, 1972, 1973, 1975, 1977, 1988. Used by permission.

© Copyright 2008, Joy of Living Bible Studies, Inc., 2500 Knoll Dr. #G, Ventura, CA 93003. Printed in U.S.A.

Any omission of credits or permissions granted is unintentional. The publisher requests documentation for future printings.

ISBN 978-1-932017-41-0

About Joy of Living

For over 35 years Joy of Living has been effectively establishing individuals around the world in the sound, basic study of God's Word.

Evangelical and interdenominational, Joy of Living reaches across denominational and cultural barriers enriching lives through the simple pure truths of God's inspired Word, the Bible.

Studies are flexible, suited for both formal and informal meetings, as well as for personal study. Each lesson contains historical background, commentary and a week's worth of personal application questions, leading readers to discover fresh insights into God's Word. Courses covering many books in both the Old and New Testaments are available. Selected courses are also available in several foreign languages. Contact the Joy of Living office for details.

Joy of Living Bible Studies was founded by Doris W. Greig in 1971 and has grown to include classes in nearly every state in the Union and many foreign countries.

Table of Contents

About Joy of Living ... 2
How to Use Joy of Living Materials ... 4

Lesson 1
Commentary: Introduction to 1 Thessalonians ... 5
Questions: 1 Thessalonians 1 ... 7

Lesson 2
Commentary: 1 Thessalonians 1 ... 11
Questions: 1 Thessalonians 2 ... 14

Lesson 3
Commentary: 1 Thessalonians 2 ... 19
Questions: 1 Thessalonians 3 ... 22

Lesson 4
Commentary: 1 Thessalonians 3 ... 27
Questions: 1 Thessalonians 4 ... 29

Lesson 5
Commentary: 1 Thessalonians 4 ... 33
Questions: 1 Thessalonians 5 ... 36

Lesson 6
Commentary: 1 Thessalonians 5 ... 41
Map: Locations mentioned in this study ... 45

How to Use Joy of Living Materials

This unique Bible study series may be used by people who know nothing about the Bible, as well as by more knowledgeable Christians. Many find a personal relationship with Jesus Christ as they study. Each person is nurtured and discipled in God's Word.

Joy of Living is based on the idea that each person needs to open their Bible and let God speak to them by His Holy Spirit, to interpret the Scripture's message in relation to that person's needs and opportunities, in their family, church, job, community, and the world at large.

Only a Bible is needed for this study series. While commentaries may be helpful, it is not recommended that people consult them before answering the daily study questions. It is most important to let the Holy Spirit lead a person through the Bible passage and apply it to his or her heart and life. If desired, the student may consult additional commentaries after answering the questions on a particular passage.

The first lesson of a series includes an Introduction to the Bible book, plus the first week's daily study questions. Some questions are simple, and some are deeper for the more advanced student. The person works through the Bible passages each day, praying and asking God's guidance in applying the truth to their own life.

For Use in a Group Setting:
After the daily personal study of the passage, the students then go to a small group where they pray together and discuss what they have written in response to the questions about the passage, clarifying problem areas and getting more insight into the passage. The small group leader helps the group focus on the Bible's truth, and not just on discussing their own problems.

After small groups meet for discussion and prayer, they often go to a large group meeting where a teacher gives a brief lecture covering the essential teaching of the Bible passage which was studied during the prior week and discussed in the small groups. The teacher may clarify the passage and challenge class members to live a more committed daily life.

At home, the student begins the next lesson, containing commentary notes on the prior week's passage and questions on a new Scripture passage.

1 Thessalonians
Lesson 1

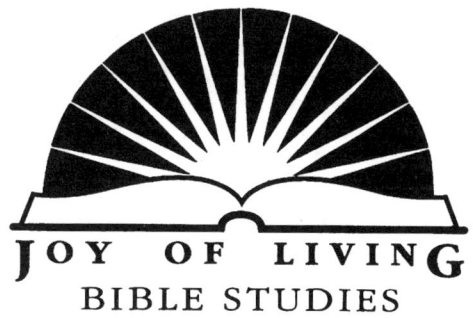

Paul, The Author

The apostle Paul, the author of this letter to the church in Thessalonica, is known as the great apostle to the Gentiles. His Hebrew name was Saul, and in the Book of Acts he was called Saul until Acts 13:9, which says, "Then Saul, who was also called Paul..." From then on in Scripture he is always called Paul, the Greek form of his name. Paul, a Jew, was a Roman citizen from birth, so he probably bore both names from an early age. The apostle always referred to himself as Paul in his letters.[1]

Paul was born near the beginning of the first century A.D., in the busy Greco-Roman city of Tarsus, located at the northeast corner of the Mediterranean Sea. There he learned his first language, Greek, was taught a trade, and received his early schooling. Growing up in a Gentile city may have helped him bridge the gap between Gentiles and Jews after his conversion to Christianity. However he was never ashamed to acknowledge himself a Jew (see Acts 21:39) and was proud of his Jewish background (see 2 Corinthians 11:22). He was the son of a Pharisee (see Acts 23:6) and was raised as an orthodox Jew. He was trained in Jerusalem under the famous rabbi Gamaliel (see Acts 22:3).

When Paul first appears in the book of Acts he is called a "young man" (Acts 7:58), and he was already an acknowledged leader in Judaism. He was intensely opposed to Christianity, and actively persecuted the followers of Jesus Christ (see Acts 26:10-11). He was convinced that Christians were heretics and that the honor of the Lord God demanded their extermination.

Paul's Conversion

The story of God's divine intervention in Paul's life is told in Acts chapter 9. Paul was on his way to Damascus, planning to arrest any Christians he found there and take them back to Jerusalem as prisoners. A light from heaven flashed around Paul, temporarily blinding him, and Jesus audibly spoke to him from heaven. Paul at once realized how wrong he was, and surrendered to Jesus' call. From that time on he served Jesus Christ and the church with all his heart.

Paul first became involved in ministry to the Gentiles in Antioch, Syria. The church in Jerusalem had sent Barnabas to Antioch to help lead the growing church there. Barnabas brought Paul to work with him in Antioch, and for a whole year they met with and taught the church there (see Acts 11:19-26). The work of Gentile foreign missions was begun by the Antioch church under the direction of the Holy Spirit when they sent Barnabas and Paul off on their first missionary journey in about 48 A.D. (see Acts 13:1-3).

Paul's Visit to Thessalonica

The apostle Paul, accompanied by Timothy and Silas, visited Thessalonica on his second missionary journey, traveling there after a tumultuous visit to Philippi (see Acts 16:12-40). Perhaps you might like to trace Paul's steps on the map on page 45.

Thessalonica is known today as Thessaloniki, the second largest city in Greece, and the capital of the Greek region of Macedonia. Cassander, king of Macedon, founded Thessalonica in 315 B.C. naming it after his wife, the sister of Alexander the Great. After the fall of the kingdom of Macedon in 168 B.C., Thessalonica became a city of the Roman Republic. It grew to be an important trade-hub located on the Via Egnatia, a Roman road that connected Byzantium (later Constantinople), with Dyrrhachium (now Durrës in Albania), facilitating trade between Europe and Asia.[2] We see the providence of God in the arrival of Christianity in Thessalonica! If Christians were settled in Thessalonica, their witness was bound to spread both eastward and westward.

In the short time he was in Thessalonica, Paul created a great stir (see Acts 17:1-10). He began by preaching in the Jewish synagogue each Sabbath, teaching that Jesus was the crucified and risen Messiah. Some of the Jews believed, as did many God-fearing Gentiles and prominent women who had been regular worshippers at the synagogue. But the unbelieving Jews caused a riot, attacking the house where the three missionaries were staying. Though Paul, Silas and Timothy were not present, the mob dragged the owner of the house and some of the other believers before the city authorities, accusing Paul and his companions of causing "trouble all over the world" (Acts 17:6).

---

1. Much of the material about the apostle Paul in this and the following paragraphs was taken from:

   J.D. Douglas, revising editor. Merrill C. Tenney, general editor. *The New International Dictionary of the Bible*. Grand Rapids: Zondervan, 1987. "Paul." 756-761.

   David Noel Freedman, editor. *Eerdmans Dictionary of the Bible*. Grand Rapids: Eerdmans, 2000. "Paul." 1016-1020.

2. "Thessaloniki." Wikipedia, The Free Encyclopedia. 2 Apr 2007, 10:17 UTC. Wikimedia Foundation, Inc. 5 Apr 2007 <http://en.wikipedia.org/w/index.php?title=Thessaloniki&oldid=119688189>.

On account of this great uproar, the Thessalonian believers sent Paul and Silas southwest to the city of Berea (see Acts 17:10). Since Timothy is not mentioned, it is possible that he stayed in Thessalonica or went back to Philippi and then rejoined Paul and Silas in Berea. More riots occurred in Berea, so Paul temporarily separated from Timothy and Silas, moving on to Athens, where he waited for Silas and Timothy to join him, and then to Corinth.

Although he spent only three weeks in Thessalonica, Paul not only founded a church there but also grounded it firmly in the faith. It was an unusual thing even in the ministry of Paul that this flourishing church should be established in less than a month! Henrietta Mears noted, "Paul's success in Thessalonica has not been the usual experience of missionaries among the heathen. Carey [William Carrey,1761-1834, British missionary and author] in India, Judson [Adoniram Judson, 1788-1850, American pioneer missionary] in Burma, Morrison [Robert Morrison, 1782-1834, British pioneer missionary] in China, Moffat [Robert Moffatt, 1795-1883, Scottish missionary, translator and father-in-law to David Livingstone] in Africa each waited seven years for his first convert. But here, the Holy Spirit allowed Paul to reap a sudden harvest."[1]

Paul wanted to revisit the church in Thessalonica, but found it impossible: "For we wanted to come to you—certainly I, Paul, did, again and again—but Satan stopped us" (1 Thessalonians 2:18).[2] However, Paul did send Timothy to strengthen and encourage the Thessalonian believers in their faith. Timothy returned to Paul in Corinth with good news about their faith and love (see 1 Thessalonians 3:1-6).

Paul's Letter

After hearing Timothy's report, Paul wrote his first letter to the Thessalonians. Timothy had discovered that there were some issues to be addressed. The Thessalonian Christians were concerned about the delay in the Lord's return. They were worried about friends who had died and feared that they would not have any part in the glory of the Lord's coming. Some of them were so overwhelmed by the truth of Christ's expected return that they had given up their jobs. They also suffered severe persecution, and were pressured to conform to the sexually promiscuous practices common in their day. Paul wrote this letter to address these things and to encourage these new converts. One of the earliest letters Paul wrote, 1 Thessalonians was probably written during the latter part of Paul's stay in Corinth around A.D. 50-51.

The major problem of the church in Thessalonica was that they misunderstood the second coming of the Lord Jesus Christ, so this was a major focus of Paul's letter. It is mentioned in the closing of every chapter: "To wait for his Son from heaven" (1 Thessalonians 1:10); "In the presence of our Lord Jesus when he comes" (1 Thessalonians 2:19); "When our Lord Jesus comes with all his holy ones" (1 Thessalonians 3:13); "Caught up together with them in the clouds to meet the Lord in the air" (1 Thessalonians 4:17); "May your whole spirit, soul and body be kept blameless at the coming of our Lord Jesus Christ" (1 Thessalonians 5:23).

Throughout history Christians have held many views about when and how Christ will return. But, as Henrietta Mears wrote, "There should be nothing doubtful or divisive about this 'blessed hope' [see Titus 2:13] of our Lord's return. No one can read the Word without finding the teaching. Let us not quarrel with one another about so sweet a message as our Lord's, 'I will come again' [see John 14:3]. This is the Christian's hope. Let us rather be watchful, for we know not the day nor the hour when the Son of man comes (see Matthew 25:13)."[3]

---

1. Henrietta C. Mears. *What the Bible Is All About* (Ventura: Regal, 1997) 542.
2. Satan has been defeated by Jesus Christ's death on the cross and His resurrection from the dead. But until Jesus returns to earth to bring about the final victory, Satan is still the prince of this world and is working against God's people.

---

3. *What the Bible Is All About*, p543.

Study Questions

Before you begin each day:
- Pray and ask God to speak to you through His Holy Spirit.
- Use only the Bible for your answers.
- Write down your answers and the verses you used.
- Challenge questions are for those who have the time and wish to do them.
- Personal questions are to be shared with the class only if you wish to share.
- As you study begin to look for a verse to memorize this week.

First Day: Read the Introduction to 1 Thessalonians.

1. What meaningful or new thought did you find in the Introduction to 1 Thessalonians or from your teacher's lecture? What personal application did you choose to apply to your life?

   Early in the book of Acts, Paul is called a "young man." (Acts 7:58) Age is not a factor when witnessing for the Lord!

2. Look for a verse in the lesson to memorize this week. Write it down, carry it with you, tack it to your bulletin board, on the dashboard of your car, etc. Make a real effort to learn the verse and its "address" (reference of where it is found in the Bible).

Second Day: Read 1 Thessalonians 1, concentrating on verses 1-2.

1. Who sent greetings to the Thessalonian Christians? (1 Thessalonians 1:1a)

   Paul, Silas, & Timothy

2. Challenge: What do you learn about Silas in the following verses? Summarize briefly.

   Acts 15:1-2, 22
   A leader among the believers

   Acts 15:36-40
   Paul's companion

3. a. Read 1 Timothy 1:2a. What does Paul call Timothy? What do you believe he meant by this?
   (A) *My true son in the faith.* (B) *Timothy was like a son - close, apprentice.*

   b. Personal: Have you ever introduced anyone to the Lord Jesus Christ, so that you are able to say, "My true son in the faith," or "My true daughter in the faith"? If not, would you like to pray now and ask God to provide opportunities to do this? Read Romans 3:23; 6:23; and 10:9-10, which will help you know what to say.

4. a. What blessing did Paul give to the Thessalonians? (1 Thessalonians 1:1b)

   Grace and peace to you.

   b. Challenge: Look up the meaning of the words "grace" and "peace" in a dictionary.
   Grace - a freely given, unmerited favor and love of God
   Peace - a state of harmony among people or groups

5. What did Paul, Silas and Timothy always do for the Thessalonian believers? (1 Thessalonians 1:2)

   Thank God for them, always mentioned them in their prayers.

6. Personal: Do you pray regularly for other believers? Do you encourage them by telling them that you pray regularly for them? Perhaps this would be a good time to begin a prayer notebook, listing people for whom you want to pray regularly.

   I could do better!

Third Day: Review 1 Thessalonians 1, concentrating on verses 3-4.

1. What did Paul, Silas and Timothy remember about the Thessalonian Christians as they prayed for them? (1 Thessalonians 1:3)

   their work produced by faith, labor prompted by love, endurance inspired by hope in Christ.

2. What does Paul say allowed the Thessalonians to exhibit these qualities? (1 Thessalonians 1:3)

3. Challenge: Read James 2:14-26. How does James show that true faith leads to actions that please God?

   faith without deeds is dead.

4. What does Paul know about the Thessalonian believers? (1 Thessalonians 1:4)

   They were chosen by God

5. How does Ephesians 1:4-5 express this same fact about all believers?

   He chose us before the creation of the world; He predestined us to be adopted — in accordance with His pleasure and will

6. Personal: God loves you and wants you to be His child by adoption through the work of Jesus Christ on the cross. Have you responded to His love and believed in Jesus Christ as your Savior?

   Yes.

Fourth Day: Review 1 Thessalonians 1, concentrating on verses 5-6.

1. In 1 Thessalonians 1:5 Paul refers to "our gospel." What do you learn in the following verses about the gospel Paul and his companions preached?

   Romans 1:16-17 *It is the power of God for the salvation of everyone who believes; It is a righteousness from God revealed*

   Galatians 1:11-12 *It is a revelation from Jesus. It is not man-made*

   2 Timothy 2:8 *Jesus Christ, raised from the dead, descended from David*

2. How did God use the words and lives of Paul and his companions to bring the Thessalonians to faith in Him? (1 Thessalonians 1:5)

   words, power, Holy Spirit, and with deep conviction

1 Thessalonians Lesson 1

3. Challenge: What did Paul say in the following verses about his preaching? Did he take the credit for leading so many to belief in Jesus Christ? No.

   1 Corinthians 1:17-18 *He preached the gospel – the message of the cross.*

   1 Corinthians 2:1-5 *He demonstrated the Spirit's power so that "your faith might not rest on men's wisdom, but on God's power."*

4. a. How did the Thessalonian believers learn to live as Christians? (1 Thessalonians 1:6a)
   through imitation

   b. Personal: If you are a Christian, is there a believer that you have imitated as you learned to walk with the Lord? Do you think there are believers that might be imitating you?
   (A) Char
   (B) yes - (Matthias) - others

5. a. What did the Thessalonians have to endure as a result of becoming Christians, and how did they respond? (1 Thessalonians 1:6b)
   severe suffering; they responded with joy given by the Holy Spirit

   b. Challenge: Read Acts 17:1-10. What example is given of the suffering the Thessalonian believers experienced? Summarize briefly.
   Jason was dragged out before everyone and forced to post bond. By doing so, Jason promised that the trouble would cease or his own property or possibly his own life would be taken.

6. Personal: Have you experienced suffering because you have followed Jesus Christ? Have you also experienced "the joy given by the Holy Spirit" in spite of your suffering? If you would like to, share with your discussion group to encourage others.
   No - Not real suffering...

Fifth Day: Review 1 Thessalonians 1, concentrating on verses 7-8a.

1. Where had the Thessalonian Christians shared their faith? (1 Thessalonians 1:7)
   Macedonia and Achaia

2. Challenge: Locate Macedonia and Achaia, the two Roman provinces into which Greece was divided, on the map on page 45. Find Thessalonica, which was a city in Macedonia.

3. Every believer is to be a model for other believers. What do you learn about this in the following verses?

   1 Timothy 4:12b *speech, life, love, faith, and purity*

   Titus 2:6-7a *do what is good. Show integrity, seriousness, and soundness of speech in one's teaching*

   (elders) 1 Peter 5:2-3 *be a shepherd of God's people, serve them, be a good example*

4. What was the result of the Thessalonians' modeling of true Christian faith? (1 Thessalonians 1:8a)
   The Lord's message "rang out" from them - BELL -

5. Personal: If you are a believer, do you realize that you are a model to others? They will judge the truth of Christ's message by your life and words. Does this seem too heavy a responsibility to you? If you are willing to depend on the Holy Spirit who lives within you, He will produce fruit in your life that will allow the Lord's message to ring out to everyone around you. Read Galatians 5:22-25. How does this encourage and challenge you to live by the Spirit?

When I live by the Spirit, the fruits of the spirit will shine in me.

Sixth Day: Review 1 Thessalonians 1, concentrating on verses 8b-10.

1. How did the Thessalonians become Christians? (1 Thessalonians 1:8b-9)

   They turned from idols to serve the living and true God.

2. The first step of true conversion is voluntarily turning away from the path one is on and turning toward the living and true God. This is called repentance. From the following verses, how does this line up with what Paul preached?

   Acts 14:15 *"turn from these worthless things to the living God..."*

   Acts 20:21 *people must "turn to God in repentance and have faith in our Lord Jesus."*

   Acts 26:17-18 *turn from darkness to light, and from the power of Satan to God, so that they may receive forgiveness of sins and a place among those who are sanctified by faith in me*

3. Whose return were the Thessalonians waiting for? (1 Thessalonians 1:10)

   Jesus

4. Challenge: What do you learn in the following verses about the coming return of Jesus Christ?

   John 14:1-3 *He will come back. (Jesus's words)*

   Acts 1:9-11 *Two men, dressed in white and from heaven, stated that He will come back in the same way He went into heaven*

   1 Thessalonians 4:16-17 *He will come down from heaven with a loud command, with the voice of the archangel and with the trumpet call of God. The dead in Christ will rise first and those still living will be caught up w/*

5. Jesus, through His death on the cross, paid for the sin of every believer and rescues us from "the coming wrath" of God against sin. What do you learn about God's coming wrath and Jesus' rescue of believers in the following verses?

   John 3:36 *belief in the Son = eternal life. No belief = wrath of God (hell)*

   Romans 1:18 *the wrath of God is being revealed against all godlessness and wickedness of men who suppress the truth*

   Colossians 3:5 *These things bring about God's wrath and need to be put away - sexual immorality, impurity, lust, evil desires and greed, which is idolatry*

6. Personal: In Paul's day, the Gentiles worshipped physical idols. Today in our culture most people do not bow down to physical idols, but are just as lost in bondage to "worthless things." Have you turned away from darkness to light, from worthless things to the true and living God? Do you look forward with joy to the return of Jesus Christ, or are you still in fear of God's judgment of your sin? Why not pray about this now?

I do look forward to His return. It's a daily struggle to overcome the "idols" of my life — busyness, TV, "things to do"

1 Thessalonians
Lesson 2

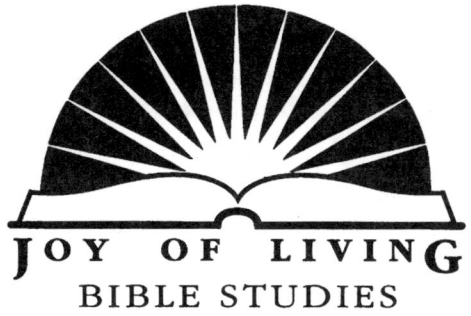

1 Thessalonians 1:1 — Paul's Greeting

As was customary in the letters of that day, Paul began his letter with his name. He included Silas and Timothy as well. These three men had founded the church in Thessalonica.

Silas was one of the leaders of the church in Jerusalem that the apostles chose to return to Antioch with Paul and Barnabas to deliver and explain the decision of Jerusalem council regarding spiritual errors (see Acts 15:1-32). Paul later chose Silas to accompany him on his second missionary journey (see Acts 15:36-40), during which time he founded the church at Thessalonica.

On this journey Paul met Timothy and invited him to accompany them. Later, Timothy was Paul's special messenger to the Thessalonian church, carrying the good news of their progress and reporting their needs to Paul at Corinth. As Henrietta Mears wrote, "We can learn much from Paul. He knew the secret of friendship so many would like to possess. He loved people... He always acknowledged others in his service and expressed appreciation for their part in every work done."[1] Do you follow Paul's pattern by loving people and acknowledging appreciation for what they do?

The letter was addressed, "To the church of the Thessalonians" (1 Thessalonians 1:1). By *church* Paul meant those people who had received Jesus Christ as Lord and Savior. These are the people who make up the church (see 1 Corinthians 12:12-13; Ephesians 1:22-23). He was not referring to a building. Paul said the Thessalonian church was "in God the Father and the Lord Jesus Christ" (1 Thessalonians 1:1). Jesus expressed it this way, in a prayer to God the Father—"I in them and you in me. May they be brought to complete unity to let the world know that you sent me and have loved them even as you have loved me" (John 17:23).

As in all his letters, Paul begins with "grace and peace" to the Thessalonians. The Greek word translated *grace* means, "Good will, loving-kindness, favor; of the merciful kindness by which God, exerting his holy influence upon souls, turns them to Christ, keeps, strengthens, increases them in Christian faith, knowledge, affection, and kindles them to the exercise of the Christian virtues."[2] It is only because of God's grace that we can have peace *with* Him. As we trust in His grace, we can have the peace *of* God in every situation that comes our way. Jesus told us, "Peace I leave with you; my peace I give you. I do not give to you as the world gives. Do not let your hearts be troubled and do not be afraid" (John 14:27). We can bask in the sunshine of God's love through our faith in the Lord Jesus Christ.

1 Thessalonians 1:2-3 — Encouragement

Next Paul said, "We always thank God for all of you, mentioning you in our prayers" (1 Thessalonians 1:2). Paul and his companions had planted the church in Thessalonica, but now they were physically separated from the Thessalonians. They continued to pray for the church, and thanked God that these dear believers were becoming spiritually mature. This maturity was evidenced in the lives of the Thessalonians, through the deeds that were the product of their faith and the love that prompted their labor.

Even their endurance through trials and persecution was evidence of their faith—they could endure only because their hope was in the Lord. The *NIV Study Bible* comments, "Our hope is not unfounded wishful thinking, but firm confidence in our Lord Jesus Christ and His return."[3]

The story is told of a young Christian who sat at the deathbed of a dear saint of God and said, "Shall I read to you the sweetest verse in the Bible?"

"Yes," said the aged saint. The young man read John 14:2, "In my Father's house are many rooms; if it were not so, I would have told you. I am going there to prepare a place for you."

"No," said the dying man, "that is not the sweetest verse. Read on." The young man read on, "And if I go and prepare a place for you, I will come back and take you to be with me that you also may be where I am." The dying man said, "That is the sweetest verse. It is not the place; it is He, Himself, I want."[4]

1 Thessalonians 1:4-6 — Loved and Chosen

In 1 Thessalonians 1:4 Paul continued, "For we know, brothers loved by God, that he has chosen you." God, out of His great love, had chosen them to be His children by faith. In the same way, God loves

---

1. *What the Bible Is All About* p544.
2. Thayer and Smith. "Greek Lexicon entry for Charis". "The NAS New Testament Greek Lexicon". <http://www.biblestudytools.net/Lexicons/Greek/grk.cgi?number=5485&version=nas>. 1999.
3. Kenneth Barker, editor. *The NIV Study Bible* (Grand Rapids: Zondervan, 1985) p1821.
4. J.R. Peniel, Herald.

you and invites you to accept His gift of salvation through Jesus Christ. Have you accepted this great gift?

Paul spoke of the Thessalonian believers as "brothers." This word points out the relationship that every Christian has with other Christians both near and far. Whoever has faith in Jesus Christ has been adopted into the family of God (see John 1:12). God accepts us into His family—not because of anything that we have done, but because the blood of the Lord Jesus Christ has covered our sins. In Ephesians 1:4-8, Paul explained this more fully, "For he [God] chose us in him before the creation of the world to be holy and blameless in his sight. In love he predestined us to be adopted as his sons through Jesus Christ, in accordance with his pleasure and will—to the praise of his glorious grace, which he has freely given us in the One he loves. In him we have redemption through his blood, the forgiveness of sins, in accordance with the riches of God's grace that he lavished on us with all wisdom and understanding."

In 1 Thessalonians 1:5 Paul stressed that the gospel (the good news of Jesus Christ) did not come to the Thessalonians only by words, but also in the power of the Holy Spirit. Although Paul was a highly educated man, he did not take the credit for converting these Gentiles from idolatry to Christianity. As he explained to the believers in Corinth, "When I came to you, brothers, I did not come with eloquence or superior wisdom as I proclaimed to you the testimony about God. For I resolved to know nothing while I was with you except Jesus Christ and him crucified. I came to you in weakness and fear, and with much trembling. My message and my preaching were not with wise and persuasive words, but with a demonstration of the Spirit's power, so that your faith might not rest on men's wisdom, but on God's power" (1 Corinthians 2:1-5). The Thessalonians were deeply convicted by the Holy Spirit of the truth of Paul's message, and their lives were changed to reflect the attitudes and actions of the Lord Jesus, as demonstrated by Paul. In spite of severe persecution, their lives were filled with the joy that only the Holy Spirit can give.

Because of God's power, the new believers became imitators of Paul and of the Lord Jesus. Paul wrote, "In spite of severe suffering, you welcomed the message with the joy given by the Holy Spirit" (1 Thessalonians 1:6).

International Christian Concern (ICC), a non-profit and interdenominational human rights organization dedicated to assisting and sustaining Christians who are victims of persecution and discrimination due to practicing their faith, reports, "Christian persecution is increasing widely thoughout Asian and African countries. Many pastors, evangelists and believers [have been] murdered, beaten and jailed. Churches [have been] vandalized"[1] There are many examples of modern-day persecution:

Converted Christian locked up in a cellar for 17 days[2]

Maheen Sathar was a strong believer in Jesus Christ for four years. But his wife Muneera did not believe in Jesus Christ. Maheen tried to convince her several times about the need of salvation, but Muneera did not even listen to him because she was influenced by her brother, Siddhiq Yasin, who is an extremist working in Riyad, Saudi Arabia.

Last month Maheen Sathar was baptized. Actually he was waiting for the baptism for a long time, because he wanted his wife Muneera to be baptized with him. At last he alone decided to take baptism. Muneera informed her brother of the baptism and immediately he traveled from Saudi Arabia. He wanted Maheen to confess back to Islam. He tried to carry him to Saudi Arabia by offering a great position. Also he offered a big house and its property as Maheen's own. But Maheen said, "Lord Jesus is far above any of the offers of this world. I may be killed, but I will never deny Jesus, for He is my Lord and Savior who granted me eternal life."

This provoked Siddhiq Yasin and his gang. They brutally beaten him in front of his wife and locked him in a cellar. They did not provide him proper food and facilities. They did not even allow Muneera to see him in the cellar. Everybody thought Maheen would change his decision and come back to Islam. But they found he is becoming stronger in the faith of Jesus day by day. So they decided to save Muneera from Maheen by killing him.

It was a shock for Muneera, for she never expected such a thought of killing would come from her brother and father. She personally prayed to God, the Almighty, accepted the Lord Jesus as her Savior and prayed for Maheen not to be harmed. Then she called Rev. Paul Ciniraj Mohamed, the Director of the Salem Voice Ministries by telephone and told him all the details. He reached the place and met the believers first… They prayed together and approached a politician. By his help they met a senior police officer and the police forcibly released Maheen from the cellar.

The same evening, a mob under the leadership of Siddhiq Yasin gathered with weapons to attack Pastor Ciniraj. Immediately some of the local people, who are secretly believing in Jesus Christ, moved him to another house. Ciniraj believes that he was protected by God because of the prayers of the children of God.

Maheen and Muneera started a new life in a new home, under the special care of the police officer. But God alone has to protect them in His mighty hands.

Believers' Homes Bulldozed in Indian Slum[3]

A Christian man was killed when members of the ruling extremist political party bulldozed 25 believers' homes in a slum in Gujarat, India. The man was run down by the bulldozer and died instantly as he tried to stop the demolition of his hut.

The slum is located on government land, but the residents have lived there for more than 20 years. The extremist members claim they bulldozed the huts as part of a government plan to expand the city, but it appears to be a blatant act of persecu-

---

1. http://www.persecution.org
2. Ibid. (April 11, 2007: Malabar, India. SVM News)
3. Ibid. [April 11, 2007: India (ANS)]

tion against the Christian residents. Many of the believers left homeless are still searching for permanent places to live. For the time being, some are living with other believers who have taken them in.

The state of Gujarat has had an anti-conversion law since 2003. This law imposes penalties of up to three years' imprisonment and a fine of 50,000 rupees ($1,000) on anyone involved in a forced conversion. The Gujarat government considers it a "forced conversion" any time someone is coerced into converting or promised something in return, like a job or healing, for changing their religion. Anyone wanting to change his religion is required to ask permission from the district magistrate, or they will face the penalties as well.

North Korean Christians Need Our Support[1]

"I experienced life in prison twice and I was also brought to a labor camp once. I stayed there for three months until, with the help of another North Korean Christian, I was released. I had to labor for 18 hours a day in the most terrible circumstances.

"The leaders of the camp only provided meals two times a day, each time a cup with 90 pieces of boiled corn. I almost died of starvation and the unbearable, heavy work. Most of the prisoners were full of hatred and complained all day, but the Christians prayed and prayed, even though they were beaten terribly and were treated worse than others.

"One time I saw a Christian lady who was martyred terribly. They beat her over and over again since she didn't stop praying. She died peacefully while praying to her Lord."

Those are the words of a North Korean Christian who survived the horrors of prison. It is believed that tens of thousands of Christians are currently suffering in North Korean prison camps. North Korea is suspected of detaining more political and religious prisoners than any other country in the world.

The communist country is characterized by a complete lack of religious freedom and of many human rights violations. For the fifth year in a row, Open Doors' World Watch List ranks North Korea as the worst violator of religious rights in the world. Christianity is observed as one of the greatest threats to the regime's power. The government will arrest not only the suspected dissident but also three generations of his family to root out the bad influence.

So we see that persecution of Christians continues in our day. While we may not currently face physical suffering as these believers in India and North Korea are experiencing, we do not know what the future will bring. We never know when the day will come that we too will know persecution. As in the days of the early church, modern-day persecuted believers find that their joy in knowing Jesus Christ far outweighs any earthly suffering. In another letter Paul wrote, "I consider that our present sufferings are not worth comparing with the glory that will be revealed in us" (Romans 8:18). Is your relationship with the Lord real? Are you filled with His joy?

1 Thessalonians 1:7-10 — Models of Faith

The Thessalonians' lives became a model to all the believers in Macedonia and Achaia—all of Greece! Everyone was talking about how God was working in and through them. The Lord's message "rang out" from them! What a great commendation from Paul.

Now Paul defines the marks of true conversion: (1) turning to God, (2) serving God, and (3) waiting for Christ to return. First, the Thessalonians "turned to God from idols to serve the living and true God" (1 Thessalonians 1:9). What a change! Serving a living God instead of going through a dead ritual that only mocked their needs by dead silence. There are many idols that people serve today. Yet, they do not consider them idols! Some of these idols are recreation, money, power, youth, hobbies, education, properties and homes, etc. None of these things are wrong in themselves until they are put ahead of serving the living God. When they get in the way of our serving God, they become idols, dead rituals, and they only mock our need for a living relationship with a living God.

Next, Paul notes that the Thessalonians are now waiting "for [God's] Son from heaven, whom he raised from the dead—Jesus, who rescues us from the coming wrath" (1 Thessalonians 1:10). In another letter Paul wrote, "The wrath of God is being revealed from heaven against all the godlessness and wickedness of men who suppress the truth by their wickedness" (Romans 1:18). God *will* judge sin—there is no question about it. In Hebrews we read, "'The Lord will judge his people.' It is a dreadful thing to fall into the hands of the living God" (Hebrews 10:30-31).

Those who believe in Jesus Christ and receive forgiveness and salvation from sin do not need to fear God's coming wrath. Jesus promised, "Do not let your hearts be troubled. Trust in God; trust also in me. In my Father's house are many rooms; if it were not so, I would have told you. I am going there to prepare a place for you. And if I go and prepare a place for you, I will come back and take you to be with me that you also may be where I am" (John 14:1-3).

Old Testament believers waited for the first coming of the Messiah long ages before He came, but at the right time Christ did come. The church has waited nearly 2,000 years for His return, and may have to wait long for Christ's promised second coming. Many have lost the vision and hope. But at the right time He will come, just as He promised.

Paul felt that the reward for all of his toil, pain and suffering would be to present these converts of his ministry to Christ when He comes again. He wrote, "For what is our hope, our joy, or the crown in which we will glory in the presence of our Lord Jesus when he comes? Is it not you?" (1 Thessalonians 2:19). Have you ever introduced anyone to the Lord Jesus Christ? Will there be a reward for you? Don't miss the joy of this experience! Pray and ask God to lead you in serving Him and sharing His good news with others.

---

1. Dr. Carl Moeller, *Christian Post*. April 10, 2007. < http://www.christianpost.com>

Study Questions

Before you begin each day:
- Pray and ask God to speak to you through His Holy Spirit.
- Use only the Bible for your answers.
- Write down your answers and the verses you used.
- Challenge questions are for those who have the time and wish to do them.
- Personal questions are to be shared with the class only if you wish to share.
- As you study begin to look for a verse to memorize this week.

First Day: Read the Commentary on 1 Thessalonians 1.

1. What meaningful or new thought did you find in the Commentary on 1 Thessalonians 1 or from your teacher's lecture? What personal application did you choose to apply to your life?

   We never know when the day will come that we too will know persecution

2. Look for a verse in the lesson to memorize this week. Write it down, carry it with you, tack it to your bulletin board, on the dashboard of your car, etc. Make a real effort to learn the verse and its "address" (reference of where it is found in the Bible).

Second Day: Read 1 Thessalonians 2, concentrating on verses 1-4.

1. a. Where had Paul, Timothy and Silas come from before visiting Thessalonica and how had they been treated? (1 Thessalonians 2:2a)

   Phillippi – suffered and insulted

   b. Challenge: Read Acts 16:12-39 and summarize how Paul and his companions were mistreated in Philippi.

   They were thrown in jail for casting a "money-making" demon from a slave girl. They were stripped and beaten for untruthful accusations and then thrown into jail. There feet were fastened in stocks

   c. Challenge: Review Acts 17:1-10a and briefly describe Paul's experience in Thessalonica.

   Jason was dragged before the city officials because he had been housing Paul and Silas. He was then forced to post bond for Paul and Silas.

2. a. Yet after all this experience how did Paul evaluate his visit to Thessalonica? (1 Thessalonians 2:1)

   It was not a failure

   b. In spite of such strong opposition how did Paul dare to tell them the gospel? (1 Thessalonians 2:2b)

   God helped them

3. How did Paul defend his ministry to the Thessalonians? (1 Thessalonians 2:3)

   It was not from error, with impure motives, nor with trickery.

4. a. Who approved Paul and entrusted him with the gospel? (1 Thessalonians 2:4a)

   God

1 Thessalonians Lesson 2

    b. Who does Paul seek to please? (1 Thessalonians 2:4b)

    God

5. Paul said that God tested his heart, his motives. What else do you learn in the following verses about God's testing of our innermost selves?

    Psalm 139:1-2

    He searches us and knows us. He knows our every move and perceives our thoughts.

    Jeremiah 11:20a

    He judges righteously and tests the heart and mind

    Hebrews 4:13

    Nothing in all creation is hidden from God's sight. We will give an account to Him who sees it all.

6. Personal: Whom are you trying to please as you go about your daily life and relationships? How might the verses you have read today change your attitude in this area? I do try to please God, however, sometimes I just try to please myself.

Third Day: Review 1 Thessalonians 2, concentrating on verses 5-8.

1. a. What did Paul say that they did not use to encourage the Thessalonians to believe in Christ? (1 Thessalonians 2:5a)

    flattery, nor a mask to cover up greed

    b. Challenge: Look up *flattery* in a dictionary.

    flatter - to try to please by complimentary speech or attention

2. What else didn't Paul do in order to advance his ministry? (1 Thessalonians 2:5b)

3. Personal: Have you ever used flattery in order to get someone to do what you desired? Have you noticed anyone doing this to you? How did it make you feel? Ask God to show you if you have behaved in this way, and to help you be honest and sincere in all your relationships.

4. a. In 1 Thessalonians 2:6a, Paul again states that they were not trying to obtain anything from the Thesssalonians. He demonstrates this in the following verses by pointing to the missionaries' behavior. What does he first point out about the rights of apostles in verse 6b?

    They were not looking for praise from the Thessalonians or anyone else, nor were they looking for finances

    b. Read 1 Corinthians 9:4-14. How does Paul demonstrate that an apostle has the right to expect financial support from those to whom he ministers? Summarize briefly.

    ?

5. Rather than asserting their rights and being a financial burden to the Thessalonians, how did Paul and his fellow missionaries act among them? (1 Thessalonians 2:7-8)

    They were gentle among them. They shared not only the gospel but also their lives

6. Personal: Are you ministering to or teaching any one? How is 1 Thessalonians 2:7-8 a good pattern to follow as you teach people of Jesus Christ and build them up in their faith? If you don't see this pattern being fulfilled in your life, why not pray and ask God to change your heart and attitude?

Matthias, kids at church

Fourth Day: Review 1 Thessalonians 2, concentrating on verses 9-12.

1. What did Paul remind the Thessalonians of in 1 Thessalonians 2:9?

   his toil and hardship, working all the time so as to not be a burden to them.

2. Read Acts 18:1-3. What was Paul's means of supporting himself?

   tentmaker

3. How does Paul again appeal to the experience of the Thessalonians in order to refute accusations against the missionaries? (1 Thessalonians 2:10)

   He says that they were witnesses, along with God, of how holy, righteous, and blameless they were.

4. Paul was not boasting about how wonderful and perfect they were, in and of themselves. Read 2 Corinthians 1:12. How does he say that they, and all believers, can be "holy, righteous and blameless"?

   Conduct themselves (ourselves) in the holiness and sincerity that are from God.

5. a. What did the apostles want the Thessalonian believers to do, and how did they express this desire to them? (1 Thessalonians 2:11-12)

   They were to live lives worthy of God. They were to be encouragers, comforters, and urge others to live likewise

   b. How is it possible to live a life worthy of God?

   Galatians 5:16 *live by the Spirit*

   Colossians 2:6-7 *live in Christ, rooted and built up in Him, strengthened in the faith, and overflowing with thankfulness.*

   1 Thessalonians 5:23-24
   keep your spirit, soul, and body blameless at the coming of our Lord Jesus Christ.

6. Personal: Do you want to live a life worthy of God? How do the verses you have read today help you understand how this is possible? If you would like to, write a prayer to God about this.

   Father, I do pray that I could live a life worthy of you! Help me to stand firm in the faith, to be rooted in you, to yearn for Christ's return, and to reach out to others until He does! Help me to walk the walk and talk the talk! In Jesus' Name, Amen.

Fifth Day: Review 1 Thessalonians 2, concentrating on verses 13-16.

1. What was the Thessalonian believers' reaction to the word of God? (1 Thessalonians 2:13)

    They accepted it as it actually is — the word of God

2. Challenge: The Word of God is mighty. What do the following verses say about it?

    A Saving Power — Romans 10:17, James 1:18 and 1 Peter 1:23

    the word of Christ
    word of truth
    living and enduring

    A Defensive Weapon — Ephesians 6:17

    sword of the Spirit

    A Probing Instrument — Hebrews 4:12

    living and active. Sharper than any double-edged sword, penetrates even to divide soul and spirit; judges the thoughts and attitudes of the heart.

    A Life Purifier — Psalm 119:9 and John 17:17

    to be pure, we must live according to your word. Your word is truth.

3. How did the Thessalonian church's experience echo that of the churches in Judea? (1 Thessalonians 2:14)

    They became imitators of God's churches in Judea, which were in Christ Jesus.

4. What had unbelieving Jews done throughout history in an effort to obstruct God's plan? (1 Thessalonians 2:14-16a)

    killed the Lord Jesus and the prophets and also drove Paul and his team out. They tried to prevent other Jews from sharing the gospel with Gentiles

5. What will certainly happen to all unbelievers, Jew or Gentile, who continue to oppose God's plan? (1 Thessalonians 2:16b)

    As they heap up their sins to the limit, the wrath of God will come upon them.

6. Personal: Have you faced hostility from unbelievers when you shared the word of God, or when you acted according to God's Word rather than according to others' expectations? Don't let this discourage you from continuing to live by God's Word and share it with others! God will have the final victory when the time is right. In the meantime, we can rest in the knowledge that He loves us and He is in control.

    laughed at / smirk / cocky attitude

Sixth Day: Review 1 Thessalonians 2, concentrating on verses 17-20.

1. Paul had fled from Thessalonica in fear of his life. How desperately did Paul want to be with the Thessalonians, and why hadn't he returned to them? (1 Thessalonians 2:17-18)

   He had an intense longing to be with them, but Satan stopped him.

2. Challenge: Satan has been defeated by Jesus Christ's death on the cross and His resurrection from the dead. But until Jesus returns to earth to bring about the final victory, Satan is still the prince of this world and is working against God's people. What do you learn about this in the following verses?

   John 16:11b *He is condemned.*

   Colossians 2:13-15 *Jesus disarmed the powers and authorities and made a public spectacle of them. He triumphed over them by the cross.*

   Ephesians 6:11-12 *We can take a stand against Satan and his schemes. He still is active even though he's defeated.*

   Revelation 12:9-10 *Satan will be "hurled down" to the earth along with his angels. He will no longer have access to God (Job 1:7). He will no longer be able to accuse people before God.*

3. What will be Paul's glory and joy when he stands in the presence of the Lord Jesus Christ at His return? (1 Thessalonians 2:19-20)

   The Thessalonians

4. Paul looked forward to standing in the presence of Jesus Christ with the proof of his faithful service to God's call. In Matthew 25 Jesus told a parable about servants whose master entrusted his property to them, before leaving on a journey. What did the master say in Matthew 25:21 to a servant who served him well?

   Well done, good and faithful servant! You have been faithful with a few things; I will put you in charge of many things. Come and share your master's happiness.

5. Personal: Do you want the Lord to be able to say this to you when you stand before Him? Is He calling you to some work right now that He wants you to be faithful in? It could be raising your family in the knowledge of God, teaching Sunday school, helping in the church office, helping someone who is sick or elderly, cooking or cleaning up for church dinners, or sharing your faith when God gives you opportunities in your office, home and community. Are you willing to pray now and give yourself completely to God, relying on the Holy Spirit to work in your life to accomplish what He is asking you to do? Do you really want to "share your master's happiness"? God is waiting for you!

   Yes!

6. Review the verse that you memorized this week. Write the verse and its address and keep it along with others you have learned in an accessible place so you can easily review your verses and grow in your spiritual treasure chest.

1 Thessalonians
Lesson 3

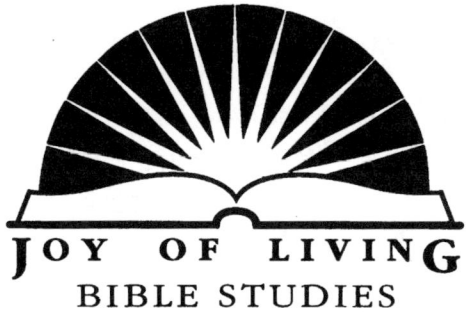

JOY OF LIVING
BIBLE STUDIES

1 Thessalonians 2:1-2 — Courage

Paul begins this section of his letter to the Thessalonians by apparently defending himself against criticism that some people had made of him after he left Thessalonica. The *International Bible Commentary* notes, "The ancient world was full of wandering 'philosophers' and 'holy men' who were greedy and unscrupulous. Some of Paul's enemies suggested that he was one of these."[1] But the Thessalonian church, through their personal experience—"You know, brothers…" (1 Thessalonians 2:1)—could testify that Paul's visit to them was productive, that he and his companions had courageously proclaimed God's message in spite of opposition and persecution.

Before Paul came to Thessalonica, he and his fellow missionaries had "suffered and been insulted in Philippi" (1 Thessalonians 2:2). In Acts 16 we read that, by order of the city magistrates, they were humiliated by being stripped of their clothes in public and beaten. Then they were thrown in prison with their feet fastened into stocks, all without a trial, to which they had a right as Roman citizens.

In spite of this past mistreatment, and knowing that the same thing could happen again in Thessalonica, Paul "dared" to preach the gospel—"with the help of our God" (1 Thessalonians 2:2). Relying on the help of God is the key! Paul was not a super-hero, able to overcome all opposition by his superior courage and abilities. He was a normal man, with normal weaknesses and fears. He said of his visit to the Corinthians, "I came to you in weakness and fear, and with much trembling." But he continued, "My message and my preaching were not with wise and persuasive words, but *with a demonstration of the Spirit's power*, so that your faith might not rest on men's wisdom, but *on God's power*" (1 Corinthians 2:3-5).

Are you ever afraid to share the gospel? Do you feel intimidated by the thought of telling an unbeliever about Jesus Christ? Remember to turn to God for His help, instead of trying to work up the courage on your own. God's power is limitless, and is available to you through His Holy Spirit that lives within you if you have accepted Christ as your Savior and Lord.

---

1. F.F. Bruce, editor. *The International Bible Commentary*. Grand Rapids: Zondervan, 1986. 1462.

1 Thessalonians 2:3-6a — Ministry and Motive

From 1 Thessalonians 2:3 it appears that there were three charges being made against Paul and his fellow missionaries:

- That the gospel they preached was based on error, being founded on human thought.
- That their teaching was prompted by impure, self-serving motives.
- That they used underhanded methods to deceive people into following their teaching.

After denying these charges, Paul went on to state positively why the charges were false. First, their message was from God. They did not make it up themselves. Second, their motive in preaching the gospel was to please God alone—not to please themselves or other people. God Himself would judge their hearts, motives, and actions. And third, they merely preached the truth and gave their listeners opportunity to respond to the truth. They did not try and sway their listeners through flattery and lies, in order to boost the number of followers and therefore boost their fame and the amount of gifts they might receive.

We can all think of "spiritual leaders" in recent times that could be charged with these same charges. Some have preached a prosperity gospel, promising automatic wealth to everyone who believes—but there is no foundation for this teaching in the Bible. Others have taken advantage of their position of authority to sexually molest women or children. And some have used gifts given to further their ministry to live a life of luxury and excess.

But Paul in this passage lays out guidelines that every person who serves the Lord ought to follow:

- Teach only God's message, not adding to it or changing it.
- Seek to please God, not yourself or other people.
- Don't be motivated by greed or impurity.
- Don't trick, flatter, lie or cover up anything.

1 Thessalonians 2:6b-9 — Sacrificial Love

Now Paul addresses the issue of financial support: "As apostles of Christ we could have been a burden to you" (1 Thessalonians 2:6b). When Jesus appointed the apostles, His primary purpose was to send them out to preach (see Mark 3:14). Apostles were entitled to be supported by the church. In 1 Corinthians 9:4-14 Paul developed a detailed explanation of this principle, concluding, "In the same way, the Lord has commanded that those who preach the gospel should receive their living from the gospel."

But because of their great love and concern for these new believers, Paul and his companions did not demand their right to financial support from them. Instead, they "worked night and day in order not to be a burden to anyone while we preached the gospel of God to you" (1 Thessalonians 2:9).

Paul was not a rich man who never had to work. Acts 18:1-3 tells us that his trade was tentmaking. When he traveled to Corinth, he lived and worked with a Jewish couple named Aquila and Priscilla, who were also tentmakers.

The apostles showed their love for the Thessalonians by being "gentle among you, like a mother caring for her little children" (1 Thessalonians 2:7). We would be shocked if a mother told her five-year-old child, "I've had it with taking care of you! You need to get out there and hustle and make some money to support me for a change." We regard parents who neglect to support and care for their little children with scorn, and remove the children from their home.

Just like the apostles, we are called to be gentle and show sacrificial love to those whom God has called us to minister to. Are you willing to give of your time and energy to people who need to see Christ in action in your life? Whether you are able to verbally share the gospel with them or not, people around you will observe your actions, your attitudes and your everyday conversation, and will make a judgment about the truth and value of your commitment to Christ. In 2 Corinthians 2:14-15 Paul wrote, "But thanks be to God, who always leads us in triumphal procession in Christ and through us spreads everywhere the fragrance of the knowledge of him. For we are to God the aroma of Christ among those who are being saved and those who are perishing." What aroma does your life spread to those around you?

1 Thessalonians 2:10-12—Blameless Behavior

Now Paul makes an amazing claim, "You are witnesses, and so is God, of how holy, righteous and blameless we were among you who believed" (1 Thessalonians 2:10). At first, that sounds egotistical, like Paul is boasting of how perfectly wonderful he and his companions are. But Paul makes it clear in many passages that he is not holy, righteous and blameless in and of himself, but only as he depends on the grace of God.

Let's look at those three words. In the Bible, *holy* means "separate, intended for a single purpose."[1] This refers to our goodness in the sight of God. Scripture says, "We have been made holy through the sacrifice of the body of Jesus Christ once for all" (Hebrews 10:10). God does this for us—we don't make ourselves holy. Once we are made holy, God desires that we live a holy life, a life according to God's design and purpose. Paul is calling on the Thessalonians to acknowledge that he and his companions had lived their lives according to God's design and purpose.

Next is *righteous*, which refers to our goodness as seen by other people. Ray Stedman said of Paul's claim to be righteous, "He behaved himself, resisting things which could be misconstrued or which would tend to mislead. In Corinthians he wrote that if his drinking wine or eating meat offended, he would not touch either again (1 Corinthians 8:13). He was righteous in his public behavior."[2]

Finally Paul says their lives were *blameless*—not sinless or perfect, but blameless. Paul and his companions had endeavored to live their lives in such a way that no charge of wrongdoing could be brought against them.

Paul loved the Thessalonians. In everything he did he endeavored to teach by example as well as by word. As he sought to live a life pleasing to God, he encouraged them to do the same. "As a father deals with his own children," Paul encouraged them, comforted them, and urged them "to live lives worthy of God" (1 Thessalonians 2:11-12).

Are you living a life "worthy of God"? Then think of younger believers that you know—perhaps a child, a grandchild, a friend or neighbor. How can you encourage, comfort and urge them to a godly life? Pray and ask God to give you His wisdom and the opportunity to minister to a young believer.

1 Thessalonians 2:13-16 — Persecution

The people of Thessalonica heard the word of God through Paul and his fellow missionaries. Though it was spoken through words of men, those who believed it knew that it was much more than that—they accepted it as the true Word of God. God gave the entire Bible to us by speaking through people. We read in Peter 1:21, "For prophecy never had its origin in the will of man, but men spoke from God as they were carried along by the Holy Spirit." And 2 Timothy 3:16 asserts, "All Scripture is God-breathed."

God's Word is a mighty instrument, Paul says, "Which is at work in you who believe" (1 Thessalonians 2:13). Ray Stedman explained, "The real Word of God always changes people and makes them different. To merely memorize or mentally accept it does not change anyone, but if people begin to act on it, to obey it, they will be permanently changed; the Word will make them into different people."[3] In the Bible, God's Word is characterized as a saving power (see Romans 10:17, James 1:18 and 1 Peter 1:23), a defensive weapon (see Ephesians 6:17), a probing instrument (see Hebrews 4:12), and a life purifier (see Psalm 119:9 and John 17:17).

When the Thessalonians believed the Word of God and it began to change their lives, the unbelievers around them took notice. Just

---

1. Ray C. Stedman. "Whatever Became of Integrity," from "Studies in First Thessalonians," Message 2. Palo Alto: Discovery Publishing, 1995. <http://www.raystedman.org/thessalonians/4090.html>.

2. Ibid.

3. Ray C. Stedman. "The Mysterious Word," from "Studies in First Thessalonians," Message 3. Palo Alto: Discovery Publishing, 1995. <http://www.raystedman.org/thessalonians/4091.html>.

like the unbelieving Jews had already done to the churches in Judea, the unbelievers in Thessalonica began to persecute the church there. The persecution carried out by the Gentiles in Thessalonica was actually instigated by unbelieving Jews (see Acts 17:5-9).

Paul notes that the present hostility toward the church by unbelieving Jews, "who killed the Lord Jesus and the prophets and also drove us out" (1 Thessalonians 2:15), is just another instance of their opposition to God's plan throughout history. In the Book of Acts, we read about Stephen, "a man full of God's grace and power, [who] did great wonders and miraculous signs among the people" (Acts 6:8). When Stephen was brought before the Sanhedrin to be judged based on the testimony of false witnesses, he preached a marvelous sermon presenting the truth to all those present. He recounted Israel's history and noted, "Was there ever a prophet your fathers did not persecute? They even killed those who predicted the coming of the Righteous One" (Acts 7:52). Scripture tells us that all unbelievers—whether Jew or Gentile—who continue to oppose God "heap up their sins to the limit" (1 Thessalonians 2:16), and are bringing the wrath of God upon themselves.

1 Thessalonians 2:17-20—Paul's Intended Visit

Again we see Paul's great love for the brothers and sisters in the church of Thessalonica. He says, "We were torn away from you for a short time (in person, not in thought)," and continues, "Out of our intense longing we made every effort to see you" (1 Thessalonians 2:17). He didn't just see them as a group of souls to be saved, and once that was done he could move on to another mission field. No, Paul loved them like a parent loves his children—deeply and unconditionally—and longed to be with them once again.

Does it surprise you to read verse 18, "For we wanted to come to you—certainly I, Paul, did, again and again—but Satan stopped us"? In our regard for Paul as a great man of God, it's easy to think that he could overcome any obstacle—how could Satan stop him? Again, we must realize that Paul was a normal human being, just like you and I. Yes, God used him mightily, but he was still subject to the same hindrances that every believer faces.

Ray Stedman gives us this insight into Satanic opposition, "The Bible is the only book that explains the persistence and malevolence of evil. Why do we struggle so in this life? What are we up against? Jesus told us that it is the devil. 'He is a liar and a murderer' ([see] John 8:44), said the Lord. He deceives and he kills. The Satanic mind is responsible for the murderous violence, the widespread deceit and false philosophies that we are confronted with today. Paul himself tells us, 'We do not wrestle with flesh and blood but with principalities and powers, the world rulers of this present darkness,' ([see] Ephesians 6:12). No other book tells you that it is not people who are your problem, but rather the spiritual forces of evil that prevail in the world."[1]

Finally, Paul explains the glorious truth about what the Thessalonian believers mean to him and to his fellow missionaries: "For what is our hope, our joy, or the crown in which we will glory in the presence of our Lord Jesus when he comes? Is it not you? Indeed, you are our glory and joy" (1 Thessalonians 2:19-20). Paul looked forward to standing in the presence of Jesus Christ with the proof of his faithful service to God's call. He not only rejoiced for the sake of the new believers—that they had been saved by grace and received God's blessings—but he also looked forward to hearing Jesus says to him, "Well done, good and faithful servant! You have been faithful with a few things; I will put you in charge of many things. Come and share your master's happiness!'" (Matthew 25:21).

Do you look forward to such a hope, joy and crown in which you will glory in the presence of Jesus when He comes? Every person that you have influenced for Christ—whether planting the seed, watering it, or harvesting it—will be your glory and joy when you stand before the Lord. Let's ask the Lord each day to give us opportunities to witness and minister in His name, and then give us the wisdom and courage to do what He desires in each situation. He will do it!

---

1. Ray C. Stedman. "The Mysterious Word," from "Studies in First Thessalonians," Message 4. Palo Alto: Discovery Publishing, 1995. <http://www.raystedman.org/thessalonians/4092.html>.

Study Questions

Before you begin each day:
- Pray and ask God to speak to you through His Holy Spirit.
- Use only the Bible for your answers.
- Write down your answers and the verses you used.
- Challenge questions are for those who have the time and wish to do them.
- Personal questions are to be shared with the class only if you wish to share.
- As you study begin to look for a verse to memorize this week.

First Day: Read the Commentary on 1 Thessalonians 2.

1. What meaningful or new thought did you find in the Commentary on 1 Thessalonians 2 or from your teacher's lecture? What personal application did you choose to apply to your life?

   see p. 20 ✱

2. Look for a verse in the lesson to memorize this week. Write it down, carry it with you, tack it to your bulletin board, on the dashboard of your car, etc. Make a real effort to learn the verse and its "address" (reference of where it is found in the Bible).

   Psalm 116:1-2

Second Day: Read 1 Thessalonians 3, concentrating on verses 1-2.

1. Where was Paul when he felt great concern for the welfare of the Thessalonian Christians? (1 Thessalonians 3:1)

   Athens

2. a. Acts 17:14 through 18:5 suggests that Paul was alone from the time when he left Thessalonica until Silas and Timothy joined him at Corinth. Read Acts 17:13-15. How did Paul come to be alone in Athens?

   Paul was preaching in Berea, and the Jews from Thessalonica stirred up the crowds. Paul was then sent to Athens and waited for Silas and Timothy to join him.

   b. What situation did Paul find in Athens that caused him great distress? (Acts 17:16)

   the city was full of idols

3. Apparently at least Timothy met Paul in Athens. Even though Paul was distressed by the idols in Athens, what did he do out of his concern for the Thessalonian church? (1 Thessalonians 3:2)

   He sent Timothy to strengthen and encourage them in their faith.

4. a. Personal: Would you be willing to be left alone if God called some member of your family or a close personal friend to a faraway mission field, or in ministry to another area of your country?

   I can only hope and pray that I would be willing to do so.

1 Thessalonians Lesson 3

b. How does Romans 10:13-15 encourage Christians to send out, support and pray for missionaries and ministers?

People are only saved when they call on the Lord. To do that, one must believe in Jesus, and that can only be done by someone telling them about Him.

5. a. What was Paul's purpose in sending Timothy to the Thessalonica? (1 Thessalonians 3:2b)

to strengthen and encourage them in their faith

b. Challenge: How do the following verses suggest that we can do the same thing for our fellow Christians today?

Galatians 6:2 Carry each other's burdens. (Share with and encourage one another)

Colossians 3:16 teach and admonish (correct) one another with wisdom that comes from the scriptures. Sing together with gratitude in your (our) hearts to God.

Hebrews 10:24-25 encourage one another in love and doing good deeds. Meet together.

6. Personal: Which of these verses has challenged you to some action which will encourage and help another person? Write down your thoughts here and then put them into action as the Holy Spirit leads you.

Galatians 6:2
Listening, encouraging, and praying for someone is so important!

Third Day: Review 1 Thessalonians 3, concentrating on verses 3-4.

1. The enemies of the Thessalonian believers may have been suggesting that their suffering proved the gospel to be false.[1] How does Paul deny this in 1 Thessalonians 3:3?

He states that they were destined for suffering.

2. Had Paul warned the Thessalonians about persecution? (1 Thessalonians 3:4)

Yes.

3. Read Acts 14:19-22, which recounts a time from Paul's first missionary journey. What did Paul say to encourage the disciples to be true to the faith in spite of persecution?

"We must go through many hardships to enter the kingdom of God."

---

1. F.F. Bruce, editor. *The International Bible Commentary*. Grand Rapids: Zondervan, 1986. 1463.

4. Challenge: In many places in the Bible, the persecution of believers is predicted. What do the following verses say about suffering for Jesus' sake?

   Matthew 5:10-12 It is a blessing. It should bring rejoicing, and sufferers should be glad. They will receive a great reward in heaven.

   John 15:18-21 Christians should expect persecution, after all, Christ was persecuted first.

   John 16:33 In this world we *will* have trouble, but Christ has overcome the world. This should bring peace to our hearts.

   2 Timothy 3:12 "Everyone who wants to live a godly life in Christ Jesus will be persecuted."

5. Personal: If you are a believer, have you experienced trials or persecution because of your faith in Jesus Christ? Did it cause you to question your faith? How do the verses you have read today help you face your current trials and prepare for future trials?

   No.

Fourth Day: Review 1 Thessalonians 3, concentrating on verses 5-6.

1. What did Paul fear in 1 Thessalonians 3:5?

   Paul was afraid that Satan may have tempted them in some way (denial of Christ?)

2. Challenge: Every believer will face temptation by Satan. Even Jesus went through this experience during His time on earth. Read Matthew 4:1-11. How did Jesus overcome each new temptation?

   "It is written..."
   He knew the scriptures!

1 Thessalonians Lesson 3

Oct/Nov. 2009

3. Personal: Jesus relied on the Word of God to overcome temptation. By doing this Bible study you are adding to your arsenal of weapons against Satan when he comes to attack your faith. Have you been memorizing a Bible verse each week? If not, will you make the effort to do it now? Hiding God's Word in your heart will strengthen you against temptation.

Psalm 116:1-2 (w/ Scott and Matthias)
I love the Lord, for He heard my voice. He heard my cry for mercy. Because ~~of His~~ He turned His ear to me, I will call on Him as long as I live.

4. Read Matthew 26:41. What else will shield the believer from temptation?

Watch and pray. (Be aware and pray!)

5. Read 1 Corinthians 10:13. What promise can we rest in when we are faced with temptation?

God is faithful and will not allow us to be tempted with more than we can bear. When we are tempted He will provide a way out.

6. How did Timothy's report put Paul's fears to rest? (1 Thessalonians 3:6)

Timothy reported that the Thessalonians were faithful and full of love. They also had pleasant memories of Paul and his team, and they longed to see Paul, etc.

Fifth Day: Review 1 Thessalonians 3, concentrating on verses 7-10.

1. How does 1 Thessalonians 3:7-8 show Paul's passionate concern for his spiritual children?

He was encouraged by their continued faith. Paul felt alive because the Thessalonians were standing firm. I think he had a sense of pride in them just as a parent has in a child.

2. What did Paul long for the Thessalonian believers to do? (1 Thessalonians 3:8b)

Stand firm in the Lord

3. Personal: Do you share this deep concern for anyone? Pray and ask God to make you a thoughtful, prayerful, concerned Christian. Make a list of people you want to ask God to give you a concern for, and begin to pray for them daily.

Matthias   Jim
Polly   Wendy
Susan   Jacob

4. Instead of patting himself on the back for a job well done, what did Paul do when he heard Timothy's report? (1 Thessalonians 3:9)

He gave thanks to God for them and for the joy he received because of their firm faith.

5. What example of consistent, caring prayer is illustrated by Paul's words in 1 Thessalonians 3:10?

"Night and day ... earnestly..."

6. Personal: Is this a challenge for your prayer life? Are you willing to set aside a time each day for prayer? Do you pray often as God brings people and their situations to your mind?

How, Lord? It's so difficult with a 4-year old who's "on the go"!

Yes

Sixth Day: Review 1 Thessalonians 3, concentrating on verses 11-13.

1. Now Paul actually prays for the Thessalonian church right in his letter. What is his first request? (1 Thessalonians 3:11)

   Paul wants to visit the Thessalonians

2. What is Paul's second request? (1 Thessalonians 3:12)

   "May the Lord make your love increase and overflow for each other and for everyone else..."

3. a. Love is the hallmark of a Christian, but we cannot make ourselves love another person. How are we able to love? Read Galatians 5:22.

   "the fruit of the Spirit" — seek and follow the Spirit's leading to bring about love.

   b. Personal: Do you find it difficult to love a certain person? Are you depending on your natural ability to lead you to love them? It is impossible to make ourselves love someone, but we can ask God to change our heart—to give us love for that difficult person (see Romans 5:5). Are you willing to ask God to change your heart and give you His love for that person? Will you pray about this now?

4. a. What is Paul's final prayer request for the Thessalonians? (1 Thessalonians 3:13)

   "May He strengthen your hearts so that you will be blameless and holy in the presence of our God and Father when our Lord Jesus comes with all his holy ones."

   b. Read Luke 9:26. How do Jesus' words show the reason for Paul's prayer request?

   If we are ashamed of Christ now, He will be ashamed of us when He returns. We are to be blameless and holy!

5. Personal: Are you ready for the second coming of Christ? If you have not yet accepted Jesus as your Savior and Lord, why not pray about it now? If you are already a believer, join Paul in prayer that God will strengthen your heart and keep you blameless and holy, ready to stand in His presence when Jesus returns.

6. Review the verse in this lesson that you memorized this week. Write the verse and its address and carry it with you.

   Psalm 116:1-2
   I love the Lord for He heard my voice. He heard my cry for mercy. Because He turned His ear to me I will call on Him as long as I live.

1 Thessalonians
Lesson 4

Nov. 11

JOY OF LIVING
BIBLE STUDIES

1 Thessalonians 3 — Introduction

As we learned in Lesson 1, when Paul and his fellow missionaries visited Thessalonica, they were blessed with many converts: "Some of the Jews were persuaded and joined Paul and Silas, as did a large number of God-fearing Greeks and not a few prominent women" (Acts 17:4). The Jews that did not believe Paul's message were jealous. They rounded up some rabble-rousers and managed to form a mob and start a riot in the city. The mob was unable to find Paul and Silas, but carried off some of the new believers to face the city officials, saying, "These men who have caused trouble all over the world have now come here, and Jason has welcomed them into his house. They are all defying Caesar's decrees, saying that there is another king, one called Jesus" (Acts 17:6-7).

That very night, the "brothers"—Thessalonian believers—immediately sent Paul and Silas away to Berea, a town about 50 miles to the southwest. But when the Jews of Thessalonica discovered that Paul was teaching the Word of God in Berea, they followed him there. Paul was delivered from their evil intentions as his Christian brothers took him to the coast and escorted him by boat to Athens. Paul sent his escorts back to Berea with instructions to Silas and Timothy to join him in Athens as soon as possible.

After Paul's companions joined him in Athens, he sent Timothy back to Thessalonica and perhaps sent Silas to some other area of Macedonia, while he, himself, stayed on alone in Athens for a time, and then later went to Corinth. After some weeks both men rejoined Paul in Corinth. Timothy was able to tell him how the Thessalonian Christians were getting along. It must have delighted Paul to hear that, rather than giving into the persecution and renouncing their faith, they were standing firm and actually sharing their faith with others! Paul was overjoyed by Timothy's good news and at once wrote a letter to congratulate and encourage these new converts. He also dealt with their practical problems, problems that are common to Christians throughout all ages.

1 Thessalonians 3:1-2—Paul's Concern

Paul knew that the young church in Thessalonica would undergo active persecution. He was very anxious about his converts' welfare and wondered if their faith would stand strong against such trials. He was especially concerned because of his sudden departure, which prevented him from giving them all of the teaching that he regarded as adequate for the establishment of the new Christian community. Yet he could not return immediately to Thessalonica, for this would only bring further persecution to these new Christians.

The spiritual atmosphere of Athens greatly distressed Paul (see Acts 17:16). Yet he cared so much for the believers at Thessalonica that he was willing to be left to preach and teach alone again in Athens for their sake. We see his affection expressed in the first verses of this chapter, "So when we could stand it no longer, we thought it best to be left by ourselves in Athens. We sent Timothy, who is our brother and God's fellow-worker in spreading the gospel of Christ, to strengthen and encourage you in your faith" (1 Thessalonians 3:1-2; Paul uses an editorial "we," referring to himself alone[1]).

Timothy was sent not just to inspect the church but also to help it! This should be the aim of every parent, teacher, preacher and friend. We are not to criticize and condemn others for their faults and mistakes. Rather, we are to show them the way out of such faults and mistakes. The Christian attitude toward the sinner or the struggler must never be that of condemnation and judgment but always that of help.

Believers today have the privilege and responsibility to strengthen and encourage one another as well. In Western culture, we are inclined toward "Lone Ranger" Christianity. Often we don't want others interfering in our lives, and we don't want to get involved in others' affairs. But Scripture instructs us, "Carry each other's burdens" (Galatians 6:2), "Teach and admonish one another with all wisdom" (Colossians 3:16), and, "Spur one another on towards love and good deeds" (Hebrews 10:24). Who is the Lord putting on your heart to strengthen and encourage? And whom will you allow to come close to you in order to strengthen and encourage you in your walk with the Lord?

1 Thessalonians 3:3-8—Persecution

Paul was anxious for his fellow Christians' spiritual welfare. On his initial visit to them he had warned them about suffering persecution. In fact, Paul regularly taught wherever he went that believers should expect trials and persecution. He wrote in a letter to Timothy, "Everyone who wants to live a godly life in Christ Jesus will be persecuted" (2 Timothy 3:12). Jesus also warned His followers of the same thing, "If the world hates you, keep in mind that it hated me first...Remember

---
1. *The NIV Study Bible*.

the words I spoke to you: 'No servant is greater than his master.' If they persecuted me, they will persecute you also" (John 15:18,20).

And Jesus *did* suffer. He was persecuted throughout His public ministry, culminating in His death on the cross for our sake. Surely if our Lord Jesus loved us this much, we should joyously and victoriously receive through His power any suffering that comes our way because of our faith in Him. Surely we can trust such a mighty Savior to turn the suffering into a blessing in His good time! Do you trust the Lord Jesus Christ in your present suffering? Remember that if you are a Christian, God never wastes anything that happens in your life, but always will work it for your good and bring glory and honor to His name. Trust Him!

Paul was anxious to find out how the Thessalonians had fared in his absence. He knew how subtle Satan's temptations could be. He said in his letter, "I was afraid that in some way the tempter might have tempted you and our efforts might have been useless" (1 Thessalonians 3:5). The Bible tells us that Satan does attack Christians. In 1 Peter 5:8 we read, "Be self-controlled and alert. Your enemy the devil prowls around like a roaring lion looking for someone to devour."

Even Jesus went through severe temptation by Satan during His time on earth (see Matthew 4:1-11). Notice what Jesus answered to every one of Satan's tempting suggestions: "It is written…" Jesus fought Satan with "the sword of the Spirit, which is the word of God" (Ephesians 6:17). Does this challenge you to renew your efforts to study and memorize Scripture verses? By hiding God's Word in your heart, you are building up your spiritual strength against Satan's inevitable attacks.

Yes, Satan does attack Christians, but God's power is far greater than any temptation that Satan may present to us. Here is a promise to rest upon: "No temptation has seized you except what is common to man. And God is faithful; he will not let you be tempted beyond what you can bear. But when you are tempted, he will also provide a way out so that you can stand up under it" (1 Corinthians 10:13). The Christian's part is to stand fast in the power of God: "Submit yourselves, then, to God. Resist the devil, and he will flee from you" (James 4:7).

Paul was greatly relieved when Timothy brought back good news of the faith and love of the Thessalonians. They were as anxious to see Paul again as he was anxious to have his fellowship restored with them! In fact, wrote Paul, "*now we really live*, since you are standing firm in the Lord" (1 Thessalonians 3:8, italics added). Do you have a personal concern for anyone like this—perhaps for a child, a grandchild, your spouse or another relative or friend? How overjoyed you would feel if you knew that person was truly walking with the Lord! That is how Paul felt.

1 Thessalonians 3:9-13—Earnest Prayer

Paul first told the Thessalonians that he and his fellow workers were so thankful to God for them—for all the joy the believers' faith and love had brought. Then he continued, "Night and day we pray most earnestly that we may see you again and supply what is lacking in your faith. Now may our God and Father himself and our Lord Jesus clear the way for us to come to you" (1 Thessalonians 3:10-11).

Even though Paul was unable to be with the Thessalonians in person, he regularly and earnestly prayed for them. Prayer is one of our spiritual weapons. In his letter to the Ephesians Paul listed the elements of the "full armor of God," with which we take our stand against the devil's schemes, ending with the most important element: "And pray in the Spirit on all occasions with all kinds of prayers and requests. With this in mind, be alert and always keep on praying for all the saints" (Ephesians 6:18).

So Paul now prayed for the Thessalonians, "May the Lord make your love increase and overflow for each other and for everyone else" (1 Thessalonians 3:12). Notice that Paul does not simply instruct the Thessalonians to make their own love grow more and more. We are incapable of manufacturing love on our own power. Love is a fruit of the Holy Spirit working within us (see Galatians 5:22). No matter how hard we try on our own to love that difficult person, it will not happen. But if we make a decision to obey Jesus' command, "Love one another. As I have loved you, so you must love one another" (John 13:34), then depend on the Holy Spirit within us to bring about this love, He will do it.

Paul's final prayer for the Thessalonians was, "May he strengthen your hearts so that you will be blameless and holy in the presence of our God and Father when our Lord Jesus comes with all his holy ones" (1 Thessalonians 3:13). In the midst of their persecution and suffering, Paul flashed the light of that wonderful day when they would be made perfect and blameless—the return of the Lord Jesus Christ in glory and victory.

Have you put your faith in Jesus Christ? Are you allowing Him to be Lord of your life, making your life pleasing unto Him? He wants to do this for every Christian, "for it is God who works in you to will and to act according to his good purpose" (Philippians 2:13). Will you allow God to work in you by the power of the Holy Spirit?

Study Questions

Before you begin each day:
- Pray and ask God to speak to you through His Holy Spirit.
- Use only the Bible for your answers.
- Write down your answers and the verses you used.
- Challenge questions are for those who have the time and wish to do them.
- Personal questions are to be shared with the class only if you wish to share.
- As you study begin to look for a verse to memorize this week.

First Day: Read the Commentary on 1 Thessalonians 3.

1. What meaningful or new thought did you find in the Commentary on 1 Thessalonians 3 or from your teacher's lecture? What personal application did you choose to apply to your life?

2. Look for a verse in the lesson to memorize this week. Write it down, carry it with you, tack it to your bulletin board, on the dashboard of your car, etc. Make a real effort to learn the verse and its "address" (reference of where it is found in the Bible).

Second Day: Read 1 Thessalonians 4, concentrating on verses 1-3a.

1. a. Paul now turns to the practical problems of Christian living. What had the Thessalonians learned from Paul during his earlier visit? (1 Thessalonians 4:1a)

    how to live in order to please God.

   b. Had the Thessalonians been following Paul's instructions? (1 Thessalonians 4:1b)

    Yes

   c. Was there room for improvement in the way they lived? (1 Thessalonians 4:1c)

    Yes

2. Why did Paul say they ought to follow the instructions he gave them? (1 Thessalonians 4:2)

    They were instructions given by the authority of Jesus

3. What does Paul say is God's will for all believers? (1 Thessalonians 4:3a)

    You should be sanctified

4. Things are sanctified when they are used for the purpose God intends. The Greek word translated "sanctification" means "holiness." *To sanctify*, therefore, means "to make holy."[1] How does 1 Corinthians 6:11b say that we are already sanctified?

    Washed and justified in the name of the Lord Jesus Christ and by the Spirit of our God.

5. Though we are already sanctified by the work of Jesus Christ, we must "become what we already are."[2] A Christian's sanctification is manifested when he or she lives according to God's design and purpose. This is what Paul was talking about back in 1 Thessalonians 4:1. How does Hebrews 12:14 express this?

    "Make every effort to live in peace with all men and to be holy; without holiness no one will see the Lord."

---

1. Elwell, Walter A. "Entry for 'Sanctification'". "Evangelical Dictionary of Theology". <http://www.biblestudytools.net/Dictionaries/BakerEvangelicalDictionary/bed.cgi?number=T625>. 1997.
2. *The International Bible Commentary* p1464.

6. Personal: Have you been washed, sanctified and justified by believing in Jesus Christ as your Savior? If you have, what is your attitude about how you live your life? Are you living to please God in all that you do, or to please yourself or other people?

I try to please the Lord, but it is too often a daily struggle against myself!

Third Day: Review 1 Thessalonians 4, concentrating on verses 3b-8.

1. a. Unlike the Jews, the Greeks had low standards of sexual morality. The believers in Thessalonica needed to live by God's standards rather than those of the surrounding culture. What instructions did Paul give in 1 Thessalonians 4:3b-5?

   Avoid sexual immorality, control your own body in a way that is holy and honorable, do not be lustful

   b. How do the following verses further explain God's standards of sexual morality?

   Romans 1:24-27 *homosexuality is wrong.*

   1 Corinthians 7:2 *One husband to one wife*

2. Many people believe that any sexual activity between consenting adults is fine—that nobody is being hurt. What did Paul add in 1 Thessalonians 4:6a that opposes this view?

   It wrongs a brother and takes advantage of him

3. What will happen to those who practice impurity and why? (1 Thessalonians 4:6b-8)

   The Lord will punish them because we are called to live a holy life. When one rejects these standards, s/he rejects God, not men.

4. Challenge: Every Christian, whether in Paul's day or today, must choose whether to live by the world's or by God's standards for sexual behavior. How do the following Scriptures encourage you to rely on God's power to help you overcome any temptation you may experience?

   1 Corinthians 10:13 *God will provide a way out of temptation*

   Hebrews 13:20-21 *Jesus equips us with everything good for doing His will*

   2 Peter 1:2-3 *By knowing Him, He provides divine power and gives us everything we need for life and godliness*

5. Personal: Have you struggled with sexual temptation or are you still struggling? Do you believe God is able to help you live by His plan? Read Mark 9:17-24. If you struggle with doubts that God can help you in this area, why not pray the same prayer that the father said to Jesus in verse 24? *no*

Fourth Day: Review 1 Thessalonians 4, concentrating on verses 9-10.

1. Who taught the Thessalonian Christians how to love each other? (1 Thessalonians 4:9)

   God

1 Thessalonians Lesson 4   31

2. The word Paul used for "brotherly love" is *philadelphia*, a Greek word that usually referred to the mutual love of children of the same father.[1] How does this word apply to Christians, according to the following verses?

   Ephesians 1:5 *We are adopted as His sons through Jesus Christ*

   1 John 3:1 *"How great is the ~~Father~~ love the Father has lavished on us, that we should be called children of God!"*

3. In 1 Thessalonians 4:9 Paul said that God had already taught the believers to love each other. Read 1 Corinthians 2:13. How does God directly teach every Christian?

   words taught by the Spirit

4. Read John 13:34-35. How did Jesus give His disciples, and therefore all believers, the same command from God?

   love one another, just as Christ loves us

5. How does Paul challenge the Thessalonians to "move forward" in their Christian love? (1 Thessalonians 4:10)

   love more and more

6. Personal: God prompts believers through His Holy Spirit within us to love our Christian brothers and sisters. But He doesn't force us to obey His prompting. We must choose to obey Him, and then He will help us love others with His love. This is why Paul could urge the Thessalonians to love all the brothers "more and more." Do you desire to obey God's command to love your fellow Christians more and more? If so, tell Him and he will help you.

Fifth Day: Review 1 Thessalonians 4, concentrating on verses 11-12.

1. What instructions did Paul give the believers in regards to their daily lives? (1 Thessalonians 4:11)

   lead a quiet life, mind your own business, and work with your hands.

2. Challenge: What is the person who is idle in danger of becoming, according to the following verses?

   2 Thessalonians 3:11-13
   busybodies

   1 Timothy 5:13
   gossips and busybodies — going from house to house

3. Personal: How do you occupy your time? If you work at a paying job, do you view it as fulfilling God's command to support yourself and any dependents you may have? If you do not need to work at an outside job for income, the ways you occupy your time still matter to God. What is your attitude about your time—do you see it as a gift from God to use for His glory, or as your own private resource to do with as you please?

   too often, yes.

4. What will be the result of living as Paul instructs? (1 Thessalonians 4:12)

   winning the respect of others, and not being dependent on anybody

5. Challenge: Believers' lives are on display for all to see. How could observing our behavior affect unbelievers, according to the following verses?

   1 Peter 2:12 *Live such a good life so they may see my good deeds and glorify God on the day (he returns) he visits us.*

---
1. *The NIV Study Bible.*

1 Peter 3:1-2

6. Personal: What message do you think your life displays to people who observe you? If you aren't pleased with this message, ask God to help use your time and act in a way that will consistently glorify Him.

Sixth Day: Review 1 Thessalonians 4, concentrating on verses 13-18.

1. Some of the Thessalonians might have misunderstood Paul and thought all believers would live until Christ returned. What was their reaction when some of them died? (See 1 Thessalonians 4:13. Note: Paul used "sleep" as a metaphor for "death.")

   great grief; grief without assurance

2. The Thessalonians wondered whether believers who had already died would share in the glory of the great day when Christ returns. What did Paul say would happen on that day to believers who had previously died, and why is this possible? (1 Thessalonians 4:14-15)

   They will be with Jesus because they knew Him. They will be ahead of those who are still living

3. Paul cited "the Lord's own word" about this matter. The specific doctrine mentioned here is not recorded in the Gospels and was either a direct revelation to Paul or something Jesus said that Christians passed on orally.[1] However, Jesus taught many times that physical death was not final for a believer. What does He say in the following verses?

   John 3:16 *Whosoever believes in Him will not perish but have everlasting life*

   John 6:54 *accepting Christ brings eternal life*

   John 11:26 *He who believes in Christ will live, even though he dies.*

4. a. How did Paul describe the return of Jesus Christ in 1 Thessalonians 4:16-17?

   The Lord will come down from heaven, with a loud command... the dead in Christ will rise first. Then, those who are alive will meet them in the air

   b. Challenge: Who will be aware of Christ's return? Do we need to be concerned about rumors of returned "messiahs"? — *no!*

   Matthew 24:30 *all nations of the earth will see him!*

   Mark 13:21 *don't believe reports of Christ's return*

   Acts 1:9-11 *He will descend from the sky*

   Revelation 1:7 *every eye will see him... all the peoples of the earth will mourn because of him*

5. What does this knowledge of Christ's return mean to Christians? (1 Thessalonians 4:18)

   Encourage one another — it's exciting, helps to keep our perspective, brings hope, prevents worry.

6. Personal: How do you feel when you think about Jesus Christ's return in power and glory? Is there someone you can encourage by talking about this with them?

   same as #5

---
1. The NIV Study Bible.

1 Thessalonians
Lesson 5

Nov. 18

1 Thessalonians 4:1-3—Live to Please God

Paul begins this chapter by saying that Christians are to live in a way that pleases God. In 2 Corinthians 5:15 he expressed it this way, "And he died for all, that those who live *should no longer live for themselves* but for him who died for them and was raised again" (italics added). We are able to live this way because God has given us a new nature. We have a choice—to live according to our old, sinful nature, or to live according to the Holy Spirit—as Paul wrote in Romans 8:5-9, "Those who live according to the sinful nature have their minds set on what that nature desires; but those who live in accordance with the Spirit have their minds set on what the Spirit desires. The mind of sinful man is death, but the mind controlled by the Spirit is life and peace; the sinful mind is hostile to God. It does not submit to God's law, nor can it do so. Those controlled by the sinful nature cannot please God. You, however, are controlled not by the sinful nature but by the Spirit, if the Spirit of God lives in you."

The term Paul uses for this change in our outlook and behavior is *sanctified*: "It is God's will that you should be sanctified" (1 Thessalonians 4:3). Things are sanctified when they are used for the purpose God intends. A human being is sanctified, therefore, when he or she lives according to God's design and purpose. The Greek word translated "sanctification" means "holiness." *To sanctify*, therefore, means "to make holy."[1]

Ray Stedman gives a helpful explanation of what *holiness* means. "When I was younger, most people thought of holiness as grimness. I did not like 'holy' people. They looked like they had been soaked in embalming fluid. They were grim and dull; they frowned on anything that was fun or pleasurable. I like the good English word *wholeness*, which also derives from the same root. Everybody wants to be a whole person. The Old Testament speaks about 'the beauty of holiness' ([see KJV] 1 Chronicles 16:29; 2 Chronicles 20:21; Psalms 29:2; 96:9), the inner attractiveness that is apparent when someone begins to function inwardly as he or she was intended."[2]

Every believer is sanctified, or made holy, when they believe in Jesus Christ as their Savior. We read in 1 Corinthians 6:11, "But you were washed, you were sanctified, you were justified in the name of the Lord Jesus Christ and by the Spirit of our God." So sanctification is accomplished entirely by the work of the Lord Jesus Christ and by His Holy Spirit working within us. In God's eyes, as soon as we believe, we are sanctified—that is an absolute fact about us.

But sanctification is also a process. As one commentator said, we must "become what we already are."[3] We must go through the process of learning to think and act in a way that pleases God. The Holy Spirit will help us in this process, but we must be willing to learn—He does not force us to think and act in a particular way, like puppets.

1 Thessalonians 4:3-8—Sexual Immorality

Paul now turns to one area with which the Thessalonians struggled, and with which every believer throughout history may struggle: human sexuality. The Thessalonians lived in a society that practiced sexual immorality, both in private life and as an expression of pagan religion. Many of the pagan temples offered prostitutes as part of worship rites. The Greeks had low standards of sexual morality, and chastity was regarded as an unreasonable restriction.[4]

In the Old Testament, God instructed His people to allow sexual conduct only within the marriage relationship (for example Exodus 20:14, Leviticus 20:10). Jesus continued this teaching, classifying sexual immorality with other sins that stem from our sinful nature: "For out of the heart come evil thoughts, murder, adultery, sexual immorality, theft, false testimony, slander" (Matthew 15:19). And He went still further, "You have heard that it was said, 'Do not commit adultery.' But I tell you that anyone who looks at a woman lustfully has already committed adultery with her in his heart" (Matthew 5:27-28). Avoiding sexual immorality is not only a matter of restraining our actions, but also our thoughts.

Paul spoke neither on his own authority nor any other man's, but "by the authority of the Lord Jesus Christ" (1 Thessalonians 4:2). We see God's authority behind this call to purity as Paul said, "It is God's will that you should…avoid sexual immorality; that each of you should learn to control his own body in a way that is holy and honorable, not in passionate lust like the heathen, who do not know God" (1 Thessalonians 4:3-4). The new life in Christ was to stand out in their society as a startling contrast to the culture of Thessalonica.

Today God calls us to this same way of life, which is a startling contrast to our culture as well. Scripture urges, "Flee from sexual im-

---

1. "Evangelical Dictionary of Theology".
2. Ray C. Stedman. "Handling your Sex Drive," from "Studies in First Thessalonians," Message 5. Palo Alto: Discovery Publishing, 1995. <http://www.raystedman.org/thessalonians/4093.html>.
3. *The International Bible Commentary,* p1464..
4. *The NIV Study Bible.*

morality. All other sins a man commits are outside his body, but he who sins sexually sins *against his own body*. Do you not know that *your body is a temple of the Holy Spirit*, who is in you, whom you have received from God?" (1 Corinthians 6:18-19, italics added). Sexually immoral conduct by a Christian violates or contaminates that which has been made sacred by the presence of the Holy Spirit.

Paul goes on to instruct, "In this matter [of sexual conduct] no one should wrong his brother or take advantage of him" (1 Thessalonians 4:6). Many people today believe that any sexual activity between consenting adults is fine—that nobody is being hurt. The fact is that sexual sin *does* harm others besides those who engage in it. Premarital sex wrongs the future partner by robbing him or her of the virginity that ought to be brought to marriage. Adultery wrongs the spouse, and also may harm the children of that union by breaking up the family.

Paul closes this topic with a sobering observation, "The Lord will punish men for all such sins, as we have already told you and warned you. For God did not call us to be impure, but to live a holy life. Therefore, he who rejects this instruction does not reject man but God, who gives you his Holy Spirit" (1 Thessalonians 4:6b-8). The believer who lives in sexual immorality is not only sinning against other people that are hurt, but against God Himself and His Holy Spirit who lives within them.

Now, what if you are an unbeliever who has lived a sexually immoral life? Or you are a Christian but have failed to control your sexual desires in a way that pleases God? Ray Stedman makes a wonderful observation:[1]

> In this day in which we live I know that probably many of you are thinking that it is too late for you; you already have messed up your lives. But the glory of the gospel is that the word is not that we must never do this; rather the word is, "Do it no longer." That is what you find all through these passages. Let us live no longer for ourselves but for "Him who loved us" and "gave himself for us" (Romans 8:37; Titus 2:14).
>
> All of us have messed up our lives in one way or another; we have destroyed the wholeness already. But the glory of the good news is that in coming to Jesus, through his work on the cross on our behalf and his raising again from the dead, he can actually give us a new start. All the past is wiped out and forgiven. We are restored. As Paul wrote, "I promised you to one husband, to Christ, so that I might present you as a pure virgin to him" (2 Corinthians 11:2). The Corinthians had already messed up their lives in many sexual ways, yet Paul declares that because they had come to Christ they were now a pure virgin.
>
> If, even as a Christian, we have messed up, the Word of God makes very clear that we can be restored. If we acknowledge that we have done wrong, and accept God's forgiveness through Christ, we are a pure virgin again in Christ. What glorious good news that is!

God has sent the Holy Spirit to give each believer victory in this area of life! We need to yield to the Holy Spirit's power and to be open to His ministry in our lives day by day (see Zechariah 4:6; Romans 8:6-14).

1 Thessalonians 4:9-10—Love Each Other

Paul urged, by God's authority, that the believers should love each other more and more. The word Paul used for this love —"brotherly love"—is *philadelphia*, a Greek work that usually referred to the mutual love of children of the same father.[2] In our flawed human relationships, we all know that brothers and sisters can fight like cats and dogs. Yet, the love of siblings for each other can also be strong and enduring. In spite of minor squabbles and irritations, blood brothers and sisters can know that they are always there for one another, ready to rejoice with one another in happy times, and to help in time of need.

How could these new Christians, who were of different cultures—Jews and Greeks—and were not related by blood, love each other like true brothers and sisters? Scripture tells us the wonderful truth—that every Christian is a child of God through adoption. Because God loved us so much, He sent His Son Jesus to die for our sins, making it possible for every believer to be adopted into His family. In Romans 8:29 we read, "For those God foreknew he also predestined to be conformed to the likeness of his Son, that he might be the firstborn among many brothers." Jesus is God's "one and only" Son (John 3:16), yet God has given us the privilege of being adopted into His family as Jesus' brothers and sisters.

Paul declared that the Thessalonians had no need for additional instruction on loving each other, because God had taught them from the beginning to do this. In Leviticus 19:18 God instructed His people through Moses, "Love your neighbor as yourself." And Jesus said, "My command is this: Love each other as I have loved you" (John 15:12). The apostle John reminded believers, "This is the message you heard *from the beginning*: We should love one another" (1 John 3:11, italics added).

God prompts believers through His Holy Spirit within us to love our Christian brothers and sisters. But He doesn't force us to obey His prompting. We must choose to obey Him, and then He will help us love others with His love (see Romans 5:5). This is why Paul could urge the Thessalonians to love all the brothers "more and more." As we submit to the Holy Spirit's leading each day, we will show forth His fruit—"love, joy, peace, patience, kindness, goodness, faithfulness, gentleness and self-control" (Galatians 5:22-23)— and become more and more like our brother and Savior, Jesus Christ.

1 Thessalonians 4:11-12—Productive Lives

If the Thessalonians were already showing brotherly love, why did Paul write to them about it again? By first pointing out and affirming their good qualities, he had a better opportunity to speak of certain deficiencies. Every Christian should learn to first affirm the good in

---

1. "Handling your Sex Drive." Scripture quotations changed to NIV.

2. *The NIV Study Bible*.

others, rather than immediately jumping into criticism. Paul elsewhere taught that a Christian's words should always be "full of grace, seasoned with salt" (Colossians 4:6). He himself told the truth, never flattered, and was always gentle (see 1 Thessalonians 2:5,7).

So Paul moved on after affirming their love for each other to give a few brief warnings. "Make it your ambition to lead a quiet life, to mind your own business and to work with your hands, just as we told you, so that your daily life may win the respect of outsiders and so that you will not be dependent on anybody" (1 Thessalonians 4:11-12). Christians are not to be restless, meddlesome loafers!

God expects believers to live productive lives, providing for our own needs and for those who depend on us. Beyond that, we are to "[help] those in trouble" and devote ourselves "to all kinds of good deeds" (1 Timothy 5:10). Those who do not do this, "get into the habit of being idle and going about from house to house. And not only do they become idlers, but also gossips and busybodies, saying things they ought not to" (1 Timothy 5:13).

Every person has the same number of hours in his or her day. We either hold our time closely to ourselves, considering it our own to do with as we wish, or we realize that every moment is a gift from God that can be used for His glory.

1 Thessalonians 4:13-18—Christ's Return

Some of the Christians had died since the Thessalonians had first heard the gospel. It appears that some of the Thessalonians misunderstood Paul's teaching and thought all believers would live until Christ returned. They were therefore worried about those who had already died. This was why Paul wrote, "Brothers, we do not want you to be ignorant about those who fall asleep, or to grieve like the rest of men, who have no hope" (1 Thessalonians 4:13). He wanted to prevent their sadness at the loss of their brothers and sisters from deteriorating into hopeless grief. In the eyes of the Greeks and the Romans death was the end of hope. Inscriptions on tombs and references in literature show that first-century pagans viewed death with horror, as the end of everything.[1] Apart from Christianity there was no hope for an after life.

In the Bible, the death of believers is often referred to as sleep. Immediately after Jesus died on the cross, Matthew 27:52 says, "The tombs were opened; and many bodies of the saints who had fallen asleep were raised" (NASB). And when Jesus heard that Lazarus was very sick, He said, "Our friend Lazarus has fallen asleep; but I am going there to wake him up" (John 11:11). Verse 13 goes on to explain, "Jesus had been speaking of his death, but his disciples thought he meant natural sleep." During the early days of the church, Stephen was martyred by stoning. Acts 7:60 relates, "Then he fell on his knees and cried out, 'Lord, do not hold this sin against them.' When he had said this, he fell asleep." The comparison of death to sleep is particularly appropriate as it implies a rest from labor as well as the glorious awakening that believers expect in heaven.

Paul made it clear that when Christ comes He will not only meet the surviving believers on earth but will also bring along with Him those who have previously died. This is made possible because Jesus died and rose again. Paul cited "the Lord's own word" about this matter (1 Thessalonians 4:15). The specific doctrine mentioned here is not recorded in the Gospels and was either a direct revelation to Paul or something Jesus said that Christians passed on orally.[2] However, Jesus taught many times that physical death was not final for a believer, that we will be raised up to eternal life on the last day (see John 6:54).

Paul gives a stirring description of Christ's return in 1 Thessalonians 4:16-17, "For the Lord himself will come down from heaven, with a loud command, with the voice of the archangel and with the trumpet call of God, and the dead in Christ will rise first. After that, we who are still alive and are left will be caught up together with them in the clouds to meet the Lord in the air. And so we will be with the Lord forever."

The greatest hope of the future is that Jesus Christ is coming again. He went away in the clouds and we were promised that He would come again in the same way (see Acts 1:9-11). He will come back in triumph and glory, and the angels will be with Him (see Matthew 25:31; Revelation 1:7). The believers of past generations will be raised, those that are alive will be changed, and thus the whole Church—those who have believed in Jesus Christ—will give a joyful welcome to the returning Savior!

"Therefore," Paul continues, "Encourage each other with these words" (1 Thessalonians 4:18). Do you think of Jesus' return with joy and anticipation? Do you talk about it with your brothers and sisters in Christ?

---

1. Ibid.

2. Ibid.

Study Questions

Before you begin each day:
- Pray and ask God to speak to you through His Holy Spirit.
- Use only the Bible for your answers.
- Write down your answers and the verses you used.
- Challenge questions are for those who have the time and wish to do them.
- Personal questions are to be shared with the class only if you wish to share.
- As you study begin to look for a verse to memorize this week.

First Day: Read the Commentary on 1 Thessalonians 4.

1. What meaningful or new thought did you find in the Commentary on 1 Thessalonians 4 or from your teacher's lecture? What personal application did you choose to apply to your life?

   We are not puppets. We must make choices — to learn, to obey, to live productive lives

2. Look for a verse in the lesson to memorize this week. Write it down, carry it with you, tack it to your bulletin board, on the dashboard of your car, etc. Make a real effort to learn the verse and its "address" (reference of where it is found in the Bible).

   Galatians 5:13

Second Day: Read 1 Thessalonians 5, concentrating on verses 1-5.

1. How does Paul describe the timing of "the day of the Lord," which will begin with the Second Coming of Christ? (1 Thessalonians 5:1-2)

   like a thief in the night (unexpected.)

2. Challenge: From the following Scriptures, who has planned Jesus' return and knows when it will take place?

   Acts 1:6-7 *the Father*

   Matthew 24:30,36 *the Father*

3. How will unbelievers experience the return of Christ? (1 Thessalonians 5:3)

   It will be suddenly as labor pains on a pregnant woman, and it will be unescapable.

4. Why will the believer's experience of the return of Christ be different than the unbeliever's? (1 Thessalonians 5:4-5)

   We long for it and expect it! (I)

5. How do Jesus' words in the following verses explain whom Paul means by the "sons of the light" and "sons of the day"?

   John 12:36 *trust in the light = trust in Christ*

   John 12:46 *Jesus has come as light into our dark world.*

   Acts 26:17-18 *those who turn from Satan to God — those who receive forgiveness of sins*

1 Thessalonians Lesson 5

6. Personal: Have you turned from the darkness to light by believing in Jesus Christ as your Savior? If not, why not pray about this now?

Yes

Third Day: Review 1 Thessalonians 5, concentrating on verses 6-11.

1. a. In 1 Thessalonians 4:13-18, Paul used the metaphor of "sleep" for physical death. But in 1 Thessalonians 5:6, "asleep" refers to spiritual insensitivity. How does Paul say believers are to be different from unbelievers in 1 Thessalonians 5:6-7?

   be alert and self-controlled

   b. Challenge: How can a Christian remain spiritually alert and self-controlled, according to the following Scriptures?

   Ephesians 6:18 *Pray in the Spirit on all occasions, be alert and keep on praying for all the saints*

   Colossians 4:2 *"Devote yourselves to prayer, being watchful and thankful."*

   1 Peter 4:7 *"be clear minded and self-controlled so that you can pray."*

2. In 1 Thessalonians 5:8 Paul uses a military metaphor to describe how a believer is equipped for spiritual battle. What spiritual assets serve as our defense against darkness and evil?

   put on a breastplate of faith and love

3. How does Paul define the hope of salvation in 1 Thessalonians 5:9-10?

   We receive salvation through our Lord Jesus Christ. He died for us so that... we may live together with Him

4. What practical use of these truths does Paul suggest in 1 Thessalonians 5:11?

   encourage one another and build each other up

5. Challenge: What do you find in 1 Thessalonians 5:6-10 that is an encouragement for you as a Christian?

   VS. 10 "He died for us so that, whether we are awake or asleep, we may live together with Him."

6. Personal: How will you use these truths to encourage and build up other believers? Think of at least one specific person that you can do this for, and plan a way to do it.

Fourth Day: Review 1 Thessalonians 5, concentrating on verses 12-15.

1. How does Paul ask believers to regard the leaders in authority in their church? Why should they do this? (1 Thessalonians 5:12-13a)

   respect them, hold them in the highest regard in love because of their work.

2. a. If Christians regard their church leaders as Paul requested, what should characterize their relationships with each other? (1 Thessalonians 5:13b)

   peaceful relationships

b. Read Philippians 2:3. What motivation will bring about this type of relationship?

"in humility consider others better than yourselves."

c. Anyone who has been a Christian very long knows how easily conflict can arise among church members. How is it possible for believers to "live in peace with each other"? Read Hebrews 13:20-21.

focus on the "God of peace." He will equip us with everything good for doing His will

3. a. How are Christians to relate to the other believers around them? (1 Thessalonians 5:14)

Warn those who are idle, encourage the timid, help the weak, be patient with everyone.

b. Challenge: What examples does Paul give in the following verses that shows what our attitude should be if we must warn another believer?

Acts 20:31 "with tears" - weeping over it, caring greatly!

1 Corinthians 4:14 think of them as "dear children" - someone loved.

1 Corinthians 10:12 be humble, not full of pride

2 Timothy 4:2 use "great patience and careful instruction."

4. a. How are we to respond to someone who has wronged us? (1 Thessalonians 5:15)

"be kind to each other and to everyone else"
"do not pay back wrong for wrong."

b. Challenge: Read Romans 12:17-21. How is the Christian response to an offense completely opposite to the way the world would respond?

Do not repay evil for evil, live at peace with everyone, do not take revenge, leave room for God's wrath, feed one's enemy, give one's enemy a drink, overcome evil with good.

5. 1 Thessalonians 5:15 presents a challenge which Christians cannot meet in their own strength. Whose strength, wisdom and love must we rely upon? Read the following verses to help you with your answer.

Romans 5:5 the Holy Spirit

Galatians 5:22-23 the Holy Spirit

Philippians 4:13 the Lord

6. Personal: Are you currently facing a wrong or offense against you? Carefully review the verses in question 5 and ask the Lord Jesus to work in your attitudes and actions so that the love of God and the power of the Holy Spirit will be seen through your response to this experience.

Fifth Day: Review 1 Thessalonians 5, concentrating on verses 16-22.

1. a. How often should a Christian rejoice? (1 Thessalonians 5:16)

   always

   b. Joy is not the same as happiness. It does not depend on our circumstances, but rather comes from what Christ has done for us. What did Jesus say in Matthew 5:11-12 that explains this? (reference = persecution)

   We are to rejoice and be glad because our reward in Heaven is great.

2. a. How often should a Christian pray? (1 Thessalonians 5:17)

   continually

   b. What should our attitude be at all times? (1 Thessalonians 5:18)

   thankful

3. Believers can follow Paul's instructions in 1 Thessalonians 5:16-18 because we know that God is in control. How does Romans 8:28 help you to understand the way to give thanks to God in difficult or even heart-breaking circumstances?

   "And we know that in all things God works for the good of those who love him, who have been called according to His purpose."

4. Personal: Have you learned to live as Paul outlines in 1 Thessalonians 5:16-18? If you find this difficult, pray and ask God to help you realize that He is all-powerful and that He is in control of all your circumstances.

5. a. What did Paul warn in 1 Thessalonians 5:19-20?

   "Do not put out the Spirit's fire. Do not treat prophecies with contempt."

   b. Challenge: Prophecy has been defined as, "the impassioned and inspired utterance of the deep things of God."[1] What do you learn about this gift of the Holy Spirit in the following verses?

   1 Corinthians 14:3 Prophets are given to strengthen, encourage, and comfort.

   Ephesians 4:11-13 Prophets are given to prepare God's people for works of service, so that the body of Christ may be built up.

6. a. Are we to accept without question the words of anyone who claims to speak in the name of the Lord? (1 Thessalonians 5:21-22)

   No. We must "test everything."

   b. Challenge: How are we to test the words of those who prophesy, according to the following verses?

   Matthew 7:15-16 We will recognize a false prophet by his fruit/results.

   Acts 17:11 examine the scripture

   2 Timothy 3:16 examine the scripture — "All scripture is God-breathed and is useful for teaching, rebuking, correcting, and training in righteousness."

---
1. *The International Bible Commentary* p1466.

Sixth Day: Review 1 Thessalonians 5, concentrating on verses 23-28.

1. Paul now prays for the Thessalonian believers. In 1 Thessalonians 5:23 who does he say is the only one that can sanctify a Christian? (Remember, *to sanctify* means "to make holy.")

    God himself

2. Why can we have confidence in Him? (1 Thessalonians 5:24)

    He is faithful ... he will do it.

3. a. What did Paul want the Thessalonians to do for him and his fellow missionaries? (1 Thessalonians 5:25)

    pray for them

    b. Challenge: From the following verses, what did Paul request prayer about? What do these requests tell you about Paul?

    2 Corinthians 1:8-11 *great hardships, life/death situations, danger*

    Colossians 4:3 *open doors to evangelize/share Christ*

    2 Thessalonians 3:1-2 *the spreading of the gospel; deliverance from wicked and evil men, for not everyone has faith*

4. Personal: Whom do you pray for? Do you care enough about them to write, telephone or visit them in person so that they realize that you are truly concerned for them?

    Susan, Polly, Jim, Wendy, Jacob

5. a. How did Paul close this first letter written in Corinth? (1 Thessalonians 5:26-28)

    Greet all the brothers with a holy kiss
    read the letter to all the brothers
    "The grace of our Lord Jesus Christ be with you."

    b. Challenge: Look up the word "grace" in a dictionary and write down its definition as though you were writing to someone and explaining what this word means to you.

    Grace — the freely given, unmerited favor and love of God
    giving what is undeserved

6. Review the verse in this lesson that you memorized this week. Write the verse and its address and keep it along with others you have learned in an accessible place so you can easily review your verses and grow in your spiritual treasure chest.

1 Thessalonians Lesson 6

Dec. 2 (handwritten)

Introduction

In 1 Thessalonians 4:13-17, Paul wrote about the Second Coming of Christ in order to comfort the Thessalonian Christians, who had recently been saddened by the death of loved ones. They might have thought all believers would live until Christ returned. Or, even if they understood that their loved ones would someday be resurrected, they thought those who had died might miss the glorious events that will surround Jesus' Second Coming. The big question was, "When and how will our bodies be resurrected?" Paul answered that when Christ returns He will bring with Him the spirits of Christians who died in ages past to be united with their risen bodies, and the Christians still alive on earth will not "precede" those who "have fallen asleep" in Jesus.

Now in chapter 5 Paul turns to a related subject, "the day of the Lord" (1 Thessalonians 5:2). The prophet Isaiah spoke of that day: "The LORD Almighty has a day in store for all the proud and lofty, for all that is exalted (and they will be humbled)... In that day men will throw away to the rodents and bats their idols of silver and idols of gold, which they made to worship. They will flee to caverns in the rocks and to the overhanging crags from dread of the LORD and the splendor of his majesty, when he rises to shake the earth" (Isaiah 2:12,20-21). *The New International Dictionary of the Bible* gives the following definition of that day:

> The day of the Lord refers to the consummation of God's kingdom and triumph over His foes and deliverance of His people. It begins at the Second Coming and will include the final judgment. It will remove class distinction, abolish sins, and will be accompanied by social calamities and physical cataclysms. It will include the millennial judgment and culminate in the new heaven and the new earth.[1]

There are many different interpretations among Christians of the Second Coming of Christ and "the day of the Lord," but do not let these differences cloud your reception of the spiritual lessons of the Bible passages. Bible scholar D. Edmund Hiebert wrote, "Equally devout and sincere students of Scripture will doubtless continue to hold different views on the question of the time... It is appropriate and proper that diligent efforts should be given to the study of the evidence for a chronology of the end time events. But these efforts must not be allowed to lead to a preoccupation with uncertain details so that the sanctifying power of this blessed hope for daily living is lost sight of."

Living with the knowledge of God's final victory gives the believer a totally new outlook on life!

1 Thessalonians 5:1-11—The Day of the Lord

Paul begins by stating, "Now, brothers, about times and dates we do not need to write to you, for you know very well that the day of the Lord will come like a thief in the night" (1 Thessalonians 5:1-2). Those who do not know the Lord will be living their daily lives, feeling secure and peaceful, and then all of a sudden disaster and judgment will come as suddenly as a woman's birth pains begin when her child is born. No one will be able to find a place to hide from God's judgment on that day.

A contrast is now drawn in 1 Thessalonians 5:4-5, "But you, brothers, are not in darkness so that this day should surprise you like a thief. You are all sons of the light and sons of the day. We do not belong to the night or to the darkness." Why won't the day of the Lord take believers by surprise? Because we should always be looking for and anticipating His return, whether through His "glorious appearing" (Titus 2:13) or our own death. The "darkness" that Paul spoke of is the darkness of sin and unbelief. The "sons of the light" are those who have faith in Jesus Christ. Because believers belong neither to night nor to darkness, sin no longer has control over them. Wrath is not in store for the Christian (see Romans 5:9). A great change has taken place: "For you were once darkness, but now you are light in the Lord. Live as children of light (for the fruit of the light consists in all goodness, righteousness and truth) and find out what pleases the Lord. Have nothing to do with the fruitless deeds of darkness, but rather expose them" (Ephesians 5:8-11).

It is true that a Christian can be disobedient to God and as a result, commit sin. The apostle John wrote, "If we say we have no sin, we deceive ourselves, and the truth is not in us. If we confess our sins, he is faithful and just, and will forgive us our sins and cleanse us from all unrighteousness" (1 John 1:8-9). A Christian should immediately confess all known sin to the Lord Jesus in order to restore his fellowship with Him, and so continue walking in the light. We may also sin unwittingly, and may not confess the sin since we are not aware of it, but Jesus' blood nevertheless cleanses us from *all* sin (see 1 John 1:7).

Paul continued his teaching in 1 Thessalonians 5:6-7: Since believers are not like those who sleep, we need to be alert and self-controlled. How can a believer be self-controlled? It is a fruit of the Holy

---
1. *The New International Dictionary of the Bible*, 259.

Spirit within us, "But the fruit of the Spirit is love, joy, peace, patience, kindness, goodness, faithfulness, gentleness and self-control" (Galatians 5:22-23).

We find a military illustration in 1 Thessalonians 5:8: "But since we belong to the day, let us be self-controlled, putting on faith and love as a breastplate, and the hope of salvation as a helmet." Paul often used the metaphor of armor in his teaching (see Romans 13:12; 2 Corinthians 6:7; 10:4; Ephesians 6:13-17). He doesn't always attach the same spiritual quality to each piece of equipment. Rather, his point is that our only hope in spiritual battles is in the qualities that God provides for us, which in this passage are faith, love, and the hope of salvation. In 2 Corinthians 10:3-4 he wrote, "For though we live in the world, we do not wage war as the world does. The weapons we fight with are not the weapons of the world."

The wonderful reason for our "hope of salvation" is given in 1 Thessalonians 5:9-10. If you have received Jesus Christ or wish to receive Him now, place your name in these verses: "For God did not appoint _Becky_ to suffer wrath but to receive salvation through our Lord Jesus Christ. He died for _Becky_ so that, whether _Becky_ [is] awake or asleep, _Becky_ may live together with him."

1 Thessalonians 5:12-15—Relationships

Apparently some members of the congregation were unwilling to respect the authority of the leaders of the church in Thessalonica. Paul said that a positive attitude toward the leaders should not only be based on respect for their position, but also on appreciation for their work. Leading a church is not an easy job! These leaders were to be models of a Christ-like life (see Hebrews 13:7; 1 Peter 5:2-3). Many ministered through preaching or teaching (see 1 Timothy 5:17). They were also responsible to warn believers of any misconduct and to oversee church discipline (see Hebrews 13:17). Paul clearly stated that Christians were to show honor to those in places of responsibility in the Lord.

Paul also cautioned the Thessalonian believers to live in peace and not quarrel among themselves. The well being of any Christian community is dependent on loving cooperation between the followers and leaders. Peace is a fruit of the Holy Spirit (see Galatians 5:22-23). The fruit of the Spirit is not the work of the believer—it is the work of Christ in the believer's soul. The apple grows on the apple tree; the orchard owner doesn't have to do it! The Lord gives increase—the fruit grows by the power of God. Peace is not merely the absence of strife; instead it is inner release from tension and it comes from Jesus Christ. When a Christian will let Christ work in him or her, the Spirit will produce His fruit in the believer. We don't need to strain, try or grit our teeth. We can relax and yield! If you have received Jesus Christ as Lord, you will find these traits growing within yourself because of your yielding to the presence of the Lord.

Paul continues, "And we urge you, brothers, warn those who are idle, encourage the timid, help the weak, be patient with everyone" (1 Thessalonians 5:14). There is no excuse for a lazy—willfully idle—Christian. As Paul later wrote to the Thessalonians, "For even when we were with you, we gave you this rule: If a man will not work, he shall not eat'" (2 Thessalonians 3:10).

But even as mature believers firmly warn the idle, we are to patiently encourage and help Christians who are timid or weak in the faith. In Romans 14:1 Paul advised, "Accept him whose faith is weak, without passing judgment on disputable matters." And in 2 Timothy 2:24-25 he instructed, "And the Lord's servant...must be kind to everyone, able to teach, not resentful. Those who oppose him he must gently instruct." Love and concern should govern every aspect of our relationships with brothers and sisters in Christ.

Paul completes this section with an instruction that is radically opposed to the way the world operates: "Make sure that nobody pays back wrong for wrong, but always try to be kind to each other and to everyone else" (1 Thessalonians 5:15). What is our first impulse, humanly speaking, when someone hurts us? We feel like striking back! But Scripture says that it's not our job to take revenge, to even the score (see Romans 12:17-21). God Himself will bring justice about, in His time.

But even knowing this, it is so hard to resist striking back, to continue to show kindness to someone who has hurt us. How can we do it? Not in our own strength! Romans 5:5 says, "God has poured out his love into our hearts by the Holy Spirit, whom he has given us." The Holy Spirit, who lives in every believer after he or she comes in faith to Jesus Christ, will produce the fruit of God's love within us. And that love is what allows us to forgive and show kindness to those who hurt us.

1 Thessalonians 5:16-22—A Rich Life in Christ

Paul certainly knew how to say a lot in just a few words! Bible teacher Henrietta Mears painted a stirring picture of Paul's concise instructions in this passage:

> While you wait [for Christ's return], Paul gives you a grand octave upon which to play great melodies of hope. Strike every note on this wonderful octave. It you do, your life will be rich.
>
> - "Be joyful always"—5:16
> - "Pray continually"—5:17
> - "Give thanks in all circumstances"—5:18
> - "Do not put out the Spirit's fire"—5:19
> - "Do not treat prophecies with contempt"—5:20
> - "Test everything"—5:21
> - "Hold on to the good"—5:21
> - "Avoid every kind of evil"—5:22[1]

You may ask, "How can I be joyful and thankful in the circumstances in which I find myself?" We often undergo painful experiences,

---
1. *What the Bible Is All About*. Scripture quotations changed to NIV.

but they can result in our spiritual eyes being opened! At first we may lash out against God, blaming Him, but the fact is that He has promised to use all the circumstance of our life for our good and His glory. He often uses such experiences to give us spiritual sight.

The key is in the instruction Paul inserts between "Be joyful" and "Give thanks"—*Pray continually*. If you constantly turn to God with your problems and fears, and give thanks for His presence and love, He will give you His peace and joy that do not depend on your circumstances. When we truly believe that God loves us, that He knows what is best for our lives, we can trust Him. It is then that we can be joyful and give thanks in the midst of difficult situations.

Many of us spend so much of our prayer time on requests, and neglect to thank God for past blessings and for those that are to come! William Barclay wrote, "There is always something, even on the darkest day, for which to give thanks. Remember that if we face the Son, the shadows will fall behind us, but if we turn our backs on the Son, all the shadows will be in front."

What did Paul mean by, "Do not put out the Spirit's fire" (1 Thessalonians 5:19)? Other Scripture passages also associate the Holy Spirit with fire. In Matthew 3:11, John the Baptist says of Jesus, "He will baptize you with the Holy Spirit and with fire." And in Acts 2:2-4, we read this description of the coming of the Holy Spirit to the twelve apostles on the Day of Pentecost: "Suddenly a sound like the blowing of a violent wind came from heaven and filled the whole house where they were sitting. They saw what seemed to be tongues of fire that separated and came to rest on each of them. All of them were filled with the Holy Spirit and began to speak in other tongues as the Spirit enabled them."

The presence of the Holy Spirit in every believer is like a fire within, a warm and glowing presence. If we know we have sinned, yet refuse to repent and confess it to the Lord, our fellowship with Him is broken and we lose the sense of the presence of His Holy Spirit. Paul wrote, "And do not grieve the Holy Spirit of God, with whom you were sealed for the day of redemption. Get rid of all bitterness, rage and anger, brawling and slander, along with every form of malice. Be kind and compassionate to one another, forgiving each other, just as in Christ God forgave you" (Ephesians 4:30-32). And the apostle John wrote, "This is the message we have heard from him and declare to you: God is light; in him there is no darkness at all. If we claim to have fellowship with him yet walk in the darkness, we lie and do not live by the truth. But if we walk in the light, as he is in the light, we have fellowship with one another, and the blood of Jesus, his Son, purifies us from all sin. If we claim to be without sin, we deceive ourselves and the truth is not in us. If we confess our sins, he is faithful and just and will forgive us our sins and purify us from all unrighteousness" (1 John 1:5-9).

In 1 Thessalonians 5:20, "Do not treat prophecies with contempt," Paul was apparently addressing the concerns of some cautious believers who had questioned the use of the spiritual gifts in the church. Scripture tells us that prophecy is a gift of the Holy Spirit (see 1 Corinthians 12:4-11; Ephesians 4:11). The *NIV Study Bible* defines *prophecy* as, "A communication of the mind of God imparted to a believer by the Holy Spirit. It may be a prediction (see Acts 11:28; 21:10-11) or an indication of the will of God in a given situation (see 1 Corinthians 14:29-30; Acts 13:1-2)."[1] First Corinthians 14:3 defines the purpose of prophecy, "But everyone who prophesies speaks to men for their strengthening, encouragement and comfort." In his letter to the Thessalonians, Paul seemed to be saying that by showing contempt for the words of the prophets, the Thessalonians were belittling the work of the Holy Spirit.

Instead of despising these prophecies, Paul continued in 1 Thessalonians 5:21, believers are to test them. Scripture gives several ways in which we can test whether a person's words are from God or not:

- *Look at the person's life.* Do they display the fruit of the Spirit (see Galatians 5:22-23)? Jesus warned us, "Watch out for false prophets. They come to you in sheep's clothing, but inwardly they are ferocious wolves. By their fruit you will recognize them. Do people pick grapes from thorn bushes, or figs from thistles?" (Matthew 7:15-16)

- *Compare the person's words to the Bible.* God does not contradict Himself. Acts 17:11 gives us an example of this type of testing, "Now the Bereans were of more noble character than the Thessalonians, for they received the message with great eagerness and examined the Scriptures every day to see if what Paul said was true."

- *Check out the person's view of Jesus Christ.* Paul wrote, "Therefore I tell you that no one who is speaking by the Spirit of God says, 'Jesus be cursed,' and no one can say, 'Jesus is Lord,' except by the Holy Spirit" (1 Corinthians 12:3). And the apostle John wrote, "This is how you can recognize the Spirit of God: Every spirit that acknowledges that Jesus Christ has come in the flesh is from God, but every spirit that does not acknowledge Jesus is not from God" (1 John 4:2-3).

1 Thessalonians 5:23-26—Paul's Prayer

At the end of this letter Paul prayed for the believers at Thessalonica: "May God himself, the God of peace, sanctify you through and through. May your whole spirit, soul and body be kept blameless at the coming of our Lord Jesus Christ." And then he reassured them, "The one who calls you is faithful and he will do it" (1 Thessalonians 5:23). The God who has called us to be sanctified—set apart for Himself—will make sure His purpose is accomplished. Sanctification is a word that can be viewed in three tenses:

- Past: We were sanctified "in Christ" when we came in faith to Him. First Corinthians 6:11 assures each believer, "You were washed, you were sanctified, you were justified in the name of the Lord Jesus Christ and by the Spirit of our God."

- Present: God continues to work in us to make us holy—set apart for Himself. Philippians 1:6 says, "He who began a good work in you will carry it on to completion until the day of Christ Jesus."

---
1. *The NIV Study Bible*. See note on 1 Corinthians 12:10.

- Future: We will be fully conformed to Christ when we see Him face to face in glory. First John 3:2 says, "Dear friends, now we are children of God, and what we will be has not yet been made known. But we know that when he appears, we shall be like him, for we shall see him as he is."

Paul then asked all of his Christian brothers and sisters to pray for him and the other missionaries in 1 Thessalonians 5:25. He and his fellow workers were people with insecurities and fears, just like the rest of us. Paul asked for prayer in many of his letters:

- "Join me in my struggle by praying to God for me. Pray that I may be rescued from the unbelievers in Judea and that my service in Jerusalem may be acceptable to the saints there, so that by God's will I may come to you with joy and together with you be refreshed." (Romans 15:30-32)

- "Pray also for me, that whenever I open my mouth, words may be given me so that I will fearlessly make known the mystery of the gospel, for which I am an ambassador in chains. Pray that I may declare it fearlessly, as I should." (Ephesians 6:19-20)

Paul ended his letter by commanding that it be read to all of the Christians in Thessalonica, for he wanted to be sure that everyone received his instruction. He then gave a benediction, a prayer for grace—Christ's continued favor and unearned love—for the Christians in Thessalonica. The apostle emphasized the majesty of Christ by using His full title—"the grace of our Lord Jesus Christ" (1 Thessalonians 5:28).

The hope and expectation of Christ's return fills Paul's first letter to the Thessalonians. And around that theme, Paul wove a message of how we are to live as we await His return. Every morning when we get up, we should ask ourselves, "Am I ready for Him to return? He might come today!" And every night we should ask, "If Jesus comes before I wake, am I ready?" What is your answer?

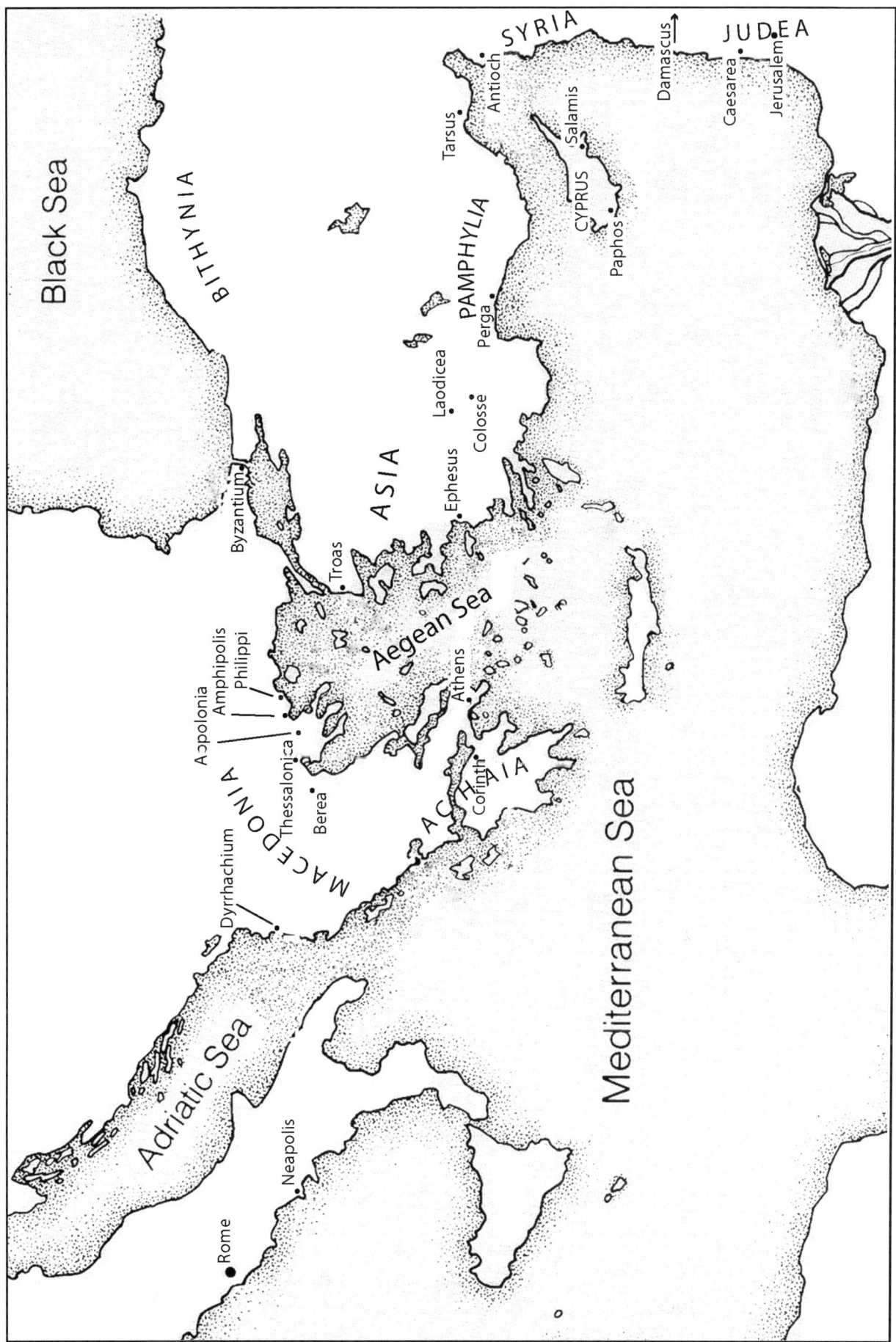

Locations mentioned in the study on 1 Thessalonians

Notes:

Notes:

Notes: